S0-BBJ-228

Learn Microsoft® FoxPro® 2.5 in a Day

For Users of Version 2.5 for DOS

Wan M. Wong

Wordware Publishing, Inc.

Library of Congress Cataloging-in-Publication Data

Wong, Wan M.
Learn Microsoft FoxPro 2.5 in a day: For Users of Version 2.5 for
DOS / Wan M. Wong.
   p. cm.
Includes index.
ISBN 1-55622-415-X
1. Data base management.   2. FoxPro (Computer file).
3. MS-DOS (Computer file).   4. PC-DOS (Computer file).
I. Wordware Publishing, Inc.   II. Title.
QA76.9.D3W6635   1994
005.75'65--dc20   93-44627
                                                              CIP

Copyright © 1994, Wordware Publishing, Inc.

All Rights Reserved

1506 Capital Avenue
Plano, Texas 75074

No part of this book may be reproduced in any form or by any means
without permission in writing from Wordware Publishing, Inc.

Printed in the United States of America

ISBN1-55622-415-X

10 9 8 7 6 5 4 3 2 1

9404

Microsoft, the Fox Head logo, FOXBASE+, FoxGraph, FoxPro, MS, and MS-DOS are registered trademarks and
Rushmore and Windows are trademarks of Microsoft Corporation in the United States of America and other
countries.

Other product names mentioned are used for identification purposes only and may be trademarks of their respective
companies.

All inquiries for volume purchases of this book should be addressed to Wordware
Publishing, Inc., at the above address. Telephone inquiries may be made by calling:

(214) 423-0090

Contents

Section 1

ABOUT THIS BOOK

INTRODUCTION

This book is for beginners. It is designed to help you get started quickly with FoxPro 2.5 for DOS. Many examples are provided to make it easy for readers to understand and use FoxPro's power tools. The examples contain step-by-step procedures to facilitate learning through doing, so readers can gain proficiency in using the tools quickly.

When you finish this book, you should be able to create and modify databases, perform queries, use multiple databases, use variables and functions, prepare printed reports, and create interactive screens and custom menu systems. In one sentence, you should become a competent end-user of FoxPro 2.5 for DOS.

ORGANIZATION

This book is organized into 14 sections which are designed to make learning both easy and engaging. The following is a brief description of each section.

Section 1—About This Book: Purpose, organization, instructional approach, and hardware and software requirements

Section 2—Database Management with FoxPro: Taking advantage of the help with FoxPro to draw the power of database management

Section 3—A Quick Start: Mastering FoxPro's interface tools to get things done easily

Section 4—Creating and Maintaining a Database: How to work with your own databases

Section 5—Browsing Your Data: How to use the Browse window for convenience and efficiency

Section 6—RQBE: Ordering and Grouping Data: Using RQBE to organize data retrieval

Section 7—RQBE: Powerful Data Retrieval: Using RQBE to retrieve data selectively from a database to provide specific information

Section 8—Reporting Made Easy: How to prepare a custom report, using the Report Writer to eliminate printer formatting chores

Section 9—Enhancing a Report: Using the Report Writer's word processing capabilities to enhance the quality of a report

Section 10—Reporting RQBE Results: Using RQBE and the Report Writer to prepare reports that are informative, organized, and good-looking

Section 11—Multiple Databases and Variables: How to use multiple databases in queries and how to perform calculations with variables in a report

Section 12—Building a Dialog Screen: Build a custom screen for displaying data and for data input

Section 13—Animating Objects on Screen: How to turn screens into communication channels between the user and FoxPro

Section 14—Creating a Custom Menu System: Creating a FoxPro-like menu system to run your applications

HARDWARE AND SOFTWARE REQUIREMENTS

FoxPro 2.5 for DOS works on an IBM or compatible personal computer (8088 or higher). It requires 640K RAM, DOS 3.1 or higher, a hard disk, a diskette drive, and a mouse.

You need a printer if you want to print your work. It can be a dot matrix or laser printer. If you do not have a printer, you can still work on all the sections in this book where printing is discussed. In this situation, you can use the screen to view the "printed" reports.

WHAT YOU SHOULD KNOW

You should be familiar with the following usage of a computer and software:

- Know how to start FoxPro from the DOS prompt.
- Understand the convention of naming disk drives, disk directories, and files.
- Understand the meaning of these DOS commands: COPY, DELETE, RENAME, and CHANGE DIRECTORY. You need not use these commands in their textual forms, however. You can reach them easily through the menus of FoxPro.

Section 2

DATABASE MANAGEMENT WITH FOXPRO

BEGINNERS WELCOME

Database management is finding wide applications in business and the work place. If you are a beginner, you need not wait to become an experienced database user before you can take advantage of database management. You actually make a start as you learn FoxPro with this book.

WHAT IS A DATABASE?

A business can use various means to keep its operation records. For example, it can keep records in paper files or in a computer system. A database is a computer-based record system. But records kept in a computer do not necessarily make a database. For example, we do not consider the text in word processing files a database. One basic feature of databases is that the data in a database can be organized in a systematic way such as a tabular format. An example of a database is a driver record system kept by a licensing authority. The information on each driver is broken down into items such as names, address, date of birth, license expiration date, and so forth. The data of every driver are stored in a standardized format. It is this systematic organization of data, applied in a computer-based system, that makes a database a distinct form of record keeping.

WHY USE A DATABASE?

A database has several notable advantages over a paper-based record system. We can mention five of them here. You can use a database to:

- Standardize collection and storage of data
- Synthesize information from the stored data
- Gain flexibility in using the stored data
- Integrate data coming from different sources
- Share data among users

DATA STANDARDIZATION   If data are to be useful, they must be collected and stored in an orderly manner. An orderly inventory of a hardware store, for example, can tell the store owner the stock levels of merchandise items in the store. Orderliness begins with standardization of data collection and storage as in a driver's license record system.

SYNTHESIS OF INFORMATION   A census is an interesting example of how much information can be synthesized from a database. The data can provide information for planning for education, urban development, employment growth, medical services, and much more. A business can use a database to synthesize information such as market trends, profitability of product lines, and product quality reviews, to name just a few.

USER FLEXIBILITY   You can standardize collection and storage of data and synthesize information from data using a paper-based record system. But you have little flexibility in using the data. Whenever you want to use part of the data, or reorganize the data to prepare an information report, you need to copy, cut, and paste the pieces of data together, *physically*. This is not a small job if you have 1,000 records. It is not a small job either to put a deck of shuffled paper records back to their original state and order. A database can handle data grouping and regrouping tasks handily and you need not worry about the data becoming disorganized.

DATA INTEGRATION   A business may have several departments such as production, sales, customer services, and accounting. Some items of data are common to many departments. Examples are the I.D.

numbers, descriptions, and stock levels of merchandise items. It is very important that the same data item reads identically across all departments, or you can expect chaos. To this end, the data common to the departments should be stored in one central system, although input data can come from different sources. For example, the stock level can be updated with data from the production department and the sales department. A database can be an effective means to integrate data in this manner.

DATA SHARING Data sharing is the opposite side of data integration. For example, if the data of the business in the previous illustration are pooled and integrated, the different departments can share the data from the central database. Data sharing can cut data processing costs and improve communications among the departments.

WHAT CAN FOXPRO DO?

FoxPro is a database management software for microcomputer use. It is the fastest software of its kind, built on an award-winning computer language technology. This software can be used to build very complex applications for real world applications such as accounting, inventory, personnel administration, statistical analysis, and information systems. To end-users, FoxPro is an effective software that can perform all essential database management functions. You can use it to:

- Create databases and store data in them
- Edit data records
- Retrieve data selectively from stored records to provide specific information
- Prepare printed information retrieval reports
- Perform calculations
- Create screens that can interact with the user
- Create menu systems to run your frequently used applications

This book teaches you how to use all these functions. As you learn the techniques, you discover how easy it is to use FoxPro.

Section 3

A QUICK START

GETTING READY

If you have not installed FoxPro, please do it now. Follow the instructions given in *Installation and Configuration* that comes with your FoxPro package. This book assumes that FoxPro is installed in D: drive in directory FOXPRO25. If the actual drive or directory name is different from the name assumed in this book, replace the assumed name with the actual name.

NOTATIONS USED IN THIS BOOK

This book uses a set of notations consistently to help you interpret the meaning of an instruction quickly. Here are the notations.

Notation	Meaning
Bold	Type the boldfaced text exactly as it appears.
italic	Data names and variable names that are used in discussion and you are not asked to type them.
ALL CAPITALS	File names, directory names, and FoxPro command words that are used in discussion and you are not asked to type them. You type them if they are boldfaced.

Notation	*Meaning (Cont.)*
Press **Key1+Key2**	Press Key1 and hold it down while you press Key2. Then release both keys. For example, **Alt+F2** means press the **Alt** key and hold it down while you press the function key **F2**. Then release both keys.
Enter	The **Enter** key on the keyboard.
Esc	The **Esc** key on the keyboard.
Arrow keys	The Up, Down, Left, Right Arrow keys.
Hot key	The highlighted letter in the prompt of a menu pad or submenu option. You can select a menu by pressing Alt+hot key, and a popup option by pressing the hot key.
Thumb	A diamond-shaped symbol on the right border of a scrollable list. You can drag the Thumb upward and downward to scroll the list.
Click	Move the mouse to point the cursor at a target, then press the left button once and release it.
Double-click	Click on a target twice in rapid succession.
Drag	Click on a target and hold down the button, move the mouse so the target moves to the desired position, then release the button.
Select	Click on a target to select it for a subsequent operation.
Deselect	Click on an empty spot of the current window to remove a previous selection of a target.

STARTING FOXPRO

If you just finished installing FoxPro, it should be up and running and you need not start it. If FoxPro was installed earlier and is not running, here are the steps to start it.

1. Go to the DOS prompt. If you need help for this step, see your DOS Users' Guide.
2. Change drive: type **D:** and press **Enter**. If you are already on D:, omit this step.
3. Change directory: type **CD\FOXPRO25** and press **Enter**. If the DOS prompt already shows D:\FOXPRO25, omit this step.
4. Type **FOX** and press **Enter**. FoxPro 2.5 should start running and the sign-on banner appears. See the following figure.

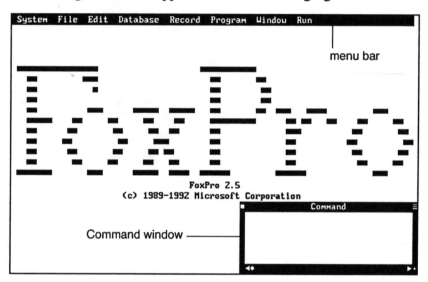

USING THE MENU SYSTEM

Your first exercise is to use the control devices to communicate with FoxPro. The control devices are collectively called the *interface*. They are applicable throughout FoxPro. Once you have learned how to use them, you can move easily in FoxPro to get things done quite effortlessly.

The menu bar is part of the interface. It is at the top of the screen. You use it to begin your selection of a function for FoxPro to perform for you. As you can see, there are eight menu pads on the menu bar. They are System, File, Edit, . . . Run. For convenience, we simply call each menu pad a menu, that is, the File menu, the Window menu, and so forth. The name of each menu clearly indicates the types of work the menu does. For example, the File menu performs tasks of file management. You do not expect the Window menu to do these tasks.

Try this to select the Window menu.

1. Click on the Window menu or press **Alt+W**. The Window menu opens. See the following figure.

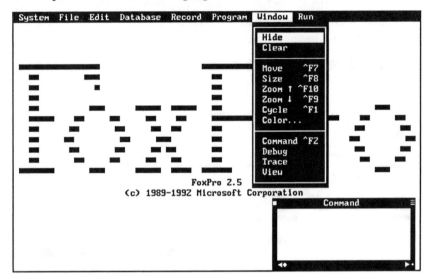

2. Click on the **Clear** option or type **R**, the hot key. (You can use lowercase.) The FoxPro banner disappears.

3. Click on the Window menu again and then click on the **Hide** option or type **H**. The Command window disappears.

TIP: A quick way to select a menu and an option on it in one combined mouse operation is to click on the menu, hold down the button, and drag the mouse until the desired option is highlighted. Then release the button.

Try this to select the File menu.

1. Click on the File menu or press **Alt+F**. The File menu opens.

2. Click on the **New** option or type **N**. A dialog appears for you to select the type of new file to open. See the following figure.

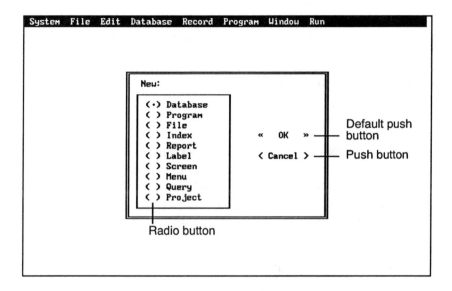

You can click on the other menu pads to view their submenus. Their names give you an idea what the menu options do. We work with selected menus in later sections of this book. To cancel the current screen, press **Esc**. Now return to the New dialog to see how to use a dialog.

USING DIALOGS

A dialog is a window displaying a variety of options for your selection. Dialogs vary with the tasks to be performed, but they are all composed of just a few types of control devices:

- Radio button
- Push button
- Popup
- List (also called scrollable list)
- Check box
- Text area

A dialog does not necessarily use all types of control devices. For example, the New dialog contains only radio buttons and push buttons. You see the other types shortly.

RADIO BUTTON   Notice from the figure that FoxPro preselects the first button for you. You can change your selection, but you can select only one radio button at any one time. Try this.

1. Click on **Query** or type **Q**, the hot key.
2. Notice that Query becomes highlighted and Database is no longer highlighted.

PUSH BUTTON   When selected, a push button usually triggers an action that you can see on the screen. For example, another dialog or screen appears. Notice the symbol which encloses OK. It means that this push button is the *default* button. You can select a default button by pressing Ctrl+Enter, regardless where the cursor is. Try this.

1. Click **OK** or press **Ctrl+Enter**.
2. Notice that another dialog appears.

We do not plan to go into this dialog at this moment. Press **Esc** to cancel it, then press **Esc** to cancel the next dialog.

TIP: Esc is a handy key. You can press it to cancel an activity you are working on. Remember, however, if you press Esc, any data you have entered during the current activity and not yet saved will be discarded.

Now select the Program menu and Compile option. A dialog appears. See the following figure. The list of files on your screen may not be identical to this figure. It depends on choices made at the time of installation of FoxPro. You can see a scrollable list, check boxes, a text area, and popups. We try each control device type in turn.

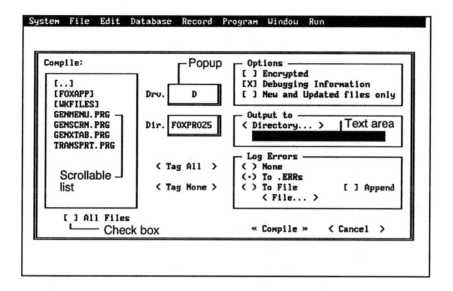

SCROLLABLE LIST   A scrollable list contains a list of options for your selection if input is required, or just for browsing if input is not required.

The scrollable list currently shows only the files with the file extension .PRG. Files of other types are excluded because you selected the Program menu and .PRG stands for "program." This list is short and you do not need scrolling, so the Thumb for scrolling does not appear. For the sake of seeing the Thumb, let us change the setting. We can do this by means of the All Files check box.

CHECK BOX   Unlike radio buttons, you can select more than one check box at the same time. When a check box is selected, an x appears inside the check box. Try this.

1. Click on **All Files** or move the cursor to the check box and press **Enter** or **Spacebar**.
2. Notice that an x appears inside the check box and the list becomes longer. Files of all types are now included on the list. The Thumb appears.
3. Scroll the list.
   a. With the mouse:
      (1) Drag the Thumb to see more of the list. Then release the button.

13

b. With the keyboard:

    (1) Press **Tab** or **Shift+Tab** to move the cursor into the list.

    (2) Press **Down** and **Up Arrow** to scroll the list.

    (3) Press **Tab** to move the cursor out of the list when done.

4. Click on **All Files**. The check box is deselected.

TEXT AREA A text area is for you to enter input data. In this dialog, it is for the name of the directory you want to send the compiled program to. Try this to enter text:

1. Click on the text area or move the cursor to it.

2. Type **B:\MYDIR** and press **Enter**.

POPUP A popup contains a list of options for your selection. The Drv. popup, for example, contains the names of the different disk drives of your computer. You can open a popup to make a selection. Try this.

1. Click on the **Drv.** popup or move the cursor to it and press **Spacebar**. The popup appears.

2. Click on **D** or press **Up Arrow** to highlight D and press **Spacebar** to select it. The popup returns to its minimized size and D: drive is selected.

3. Notice that the files now displayed are those on your D: drive.

We do not plan to go any further with the Compile dialog. Press **Esc** to discard the selections. The dialog closes.

HANDLING THE SYSTEM WINDOW

The System window can be used in many applications. An example is the Command window which is built on the System window. Let us bring back the Command window to try the features of the System window.

1. Click on the Window menu or press **Alt+W**.

2. Click on the **Command** option or press **Down Arrow** to highlight it and then press **Enter**. The Command window appears.

3. Use the following figure to identify the features of the System window.

TIP: You can bring back the Command window by pressing **Ctrl+F2**.

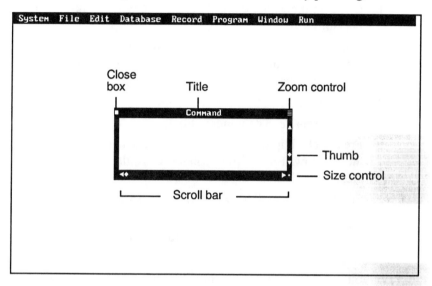

MOVE THE WINDOW   You can move the window. This feature can be useful if the window is blocking some area of display of another window at the back.

1. With the mouse:
   a. Click on the title bar of the window and drag the window to the desired position on the screen.
   b. Release the button.
2. With the keyboard:
   a. Press **Alt+W** to open the Window menu.
   b. Press **Ctrl+F7** (Move). The Command window blinks.
   c. Press **Left, Right, Up,** or **Down Arrow** to move the window to the desired position.
   d. Press **Enter** to fix the window position. The blinking stops.

CHANGE THE WINDOW SIZE   You can maximize the size of the window to cover the entire screen. You can minimize it to one line. Or you can change the size to some value in between. Try this:

1. With the mouse:

   a. Click on the Zoom control. The window enlarges to cover the entire screen.

   b. Click on the Zoom control again. The window returns to its previous size.

   c. Click on the Size control. Drag the mouse to enlarge or shrink the window. Release the button when the window has the desired size.

2. With the keyboard:

   a. Press **Ctrl+F8**. The window blinks.

   b. Press **Left, Right, Down,** or **Up Arrow** to enlarge or shrink the window. Press **Enter** when the window has the desired size. The blinking stops.

   c. Press **Ctrl+F10**. The window enlarges to cover the entire screen.

   d. Press **Ctrl+F10** again. The window returns to its previous size.

TIP: If you forget which key to press, you can find the keyboard options in the Window menu.

3. Click on the Close box or press **Alt+W** and select **Hide** to hide the Command window when done.

CREATING A WORK FILE SUBDIRECTORY

You are going to create your own files. It is good practice to create a subdirectory to hold your files, separate from the FoxPro files. That way, you can easily identify your own files and you do not accidentally erase or change a FoxPro file. If you like this idea, you can create a subdirectory off the directory FOXPRO25. Let us call this subdirectory D:\FOXPRO25\WKFILES. You can use some other name if you want and modify the name used in this book as necessary.

Follow these steps to make the subdirectory.

1. Press **Ctrl+F2** to bring back the Command window.

2. Type **RUN MD\FOXPRO25\WKFILES** and press **Enter**. Be sure to include the blank spaces between the words. FoxPro

disappears for a moment and then returns. The subdirectory WKFILES is made. You can use it in the next task.

COPYING COMPANION DISKETTE TO WKFILES SUBDIRECTORY

Copy all the files on the companion diskette supplied with this book to the work file subdirectory. Here are the steps to follow.

1. Insert the companion diskette in drive A: and close the drive.

2. Type **RUN COPY A:*.* D:\FOXPRO25\WKFILES** and press **Enter**. If you use other drives or other directories, then change the names assumed in this step with the actual names. Notice that DOS echoes to the monitor screen the files it is copying.

3. Wait until the cursor blinks in the Command window again.

4. Type **CLEAR** and press **Enter** to restore the color of the monitor.

5. Type **SET DEFAULT TO D:\FOXPRO25\WKFILES** and press **Enter**. This command asks FoxPro to use the subdirectory as the current default directory.

TIP: This command will remain in effect until you exit from FoxPro or you change the setting with another SET DEFAULT command. Next time you work on FoxPro, you need to issue the same command again. An alternative to using SET DEFAULT is to create a simple batch file to run FoxPro in the directory FOXPRO25\WKFILES.

6. Click on the Close box or press **Alt+W** and then type **H** to close the Command window.

You have done an important exercise and you and FoxPro are no longer a stranger to each other. You deserve a break, and when you return, you will work with FoxPro to create your own database.

Section 4

CREATING AND MAINTAINING A DATABASE

INTRODUCTION

A database management system may consist of one or more data files each called a database. A frequent task of an end-user of a database management system is to maintain existing databases. An end-user may also create his or her own databases and work with them. This section prepares you for these tasks. In this section, you learn how to:

- Create a database structure
- Save the new file
- Add records to the file
- Change the contents of existing records
- Delete existing records
- Modify a database structure

UNDERSTANDING DATABASE STRUCTURE

Let us suppose that you have to create a database for a firm which gives seminars to clients. The firm wants to use the data for preparing mailing lists of promotional brochures targeted at clients of different occupational categories. The firm also wants to use the data to track clients' attendance at its seminars. The attendance is a good indicator of clients' interest in the firm's seminars.

A database is made up of a series of records. The format of all the records is identical. Information about each client is stored in a separate record. It is important that the information is broken down systematically into items or *fields* so that you can successfully retrieve the stored information when needed. Information retrieval is the most important consideration in determining how to organize a database. According to the purposes of the example database, the database structure may consist of 13 fields:

Last name	Other names	Client I.D. number
Occupational cat.	Position title	Employer company
Employer address	City	State
Zip code	No. of seminars attended	
Date of last seminar	Notes	

Is there a good reason to break down a client's name into two parts, namely, the last name and other names? Yes. You have noted that a database must be designed for information retrieval. Suppose you want to retrieve information about a client whose last name is "Smith," then all you need to do is to search the last name field of the records to match this name. You need not go through other information in the records during the search. This will speed up the search. Similarly, if the firm wants to send brochures to clients of a certain occupational category, you can easily pick the correct clients by searching the occupational category field.

Each field of the database structure is defined by four parameters: the field name, type, width, and index.

FIELD NAMES   Each field must have a unique name for its proper identification. There are a few rules governing a field name:

- It must contain no more than 10 characters. The characters may be chosen from the letters a. . .z, the numerals 0. . .9, and the underscore (_).
- The first character must be a letter.
- A blank space is not allowed as part of a name.
- The letters may be in uppercase or lowercase.

It is good practice to coin a name that meaningfully indicates the nature of the contents of the field. Do not use words that are FoxPro command words, for example, ALL, DATE, to avoid confusion. If you are not sure which word is a command word, coin names that are unique.

For the example database, you can use the field names shown in the following table.

	Field Name	Description
1	*lastname*	Last name of client
2	*morename*	Other names of client
3	*id_num*	I.D. number of client
4	*jobtype*	Occupational category
5	*title*	Position title
6	*employer*	Employer company name
7	*street*	Employer street address
8	*city*	City name of address
9	*state*	State abbreviation
10	*zip*	Zip code of address
11	*howmany*	No. of seminars attended
12	*lastdate*	Date of last seminar
13	*notepad*	Memo field for notes

FIELD TYPES AND WIDTHS These two parameters work closely together. The field type determines the type of data that you can enter. The field width determines how much space will be allocated for storing the data.

FoxPro offers six field types which are shown in the following table.

Field Type	Field Width	Best Used For
Character	Max. 254 char. Default 10	Names, codes, book titles, etc.
Numeric	Max. 20 char. Default 8	Calculation
Float	Same as numeric	Calculation
Logical	1 char.	Answering yes, no, true, or false
Date	8 char.	Date of action. Example: date of hire
Memo	Any length	Descriptive text. Example: description of merchandise

Character This field can accept any printable character including the blank. Notice that uppercase and lowercase characters are normally treated as different from each other. If you want to use numerals as text, you can designate them as character fields.

Numeric This field can include a decimal point. The data can be an integer (no decimal value, for example 3), or a noninteger (with a decimal value, for example 3.21). It can also be positive or negative. A negative value must begin with a negative sign (–), for example –3.21.

Float This field is similar to the numeric field type but is often used for scientific calculation.

Logical The value of this field must be one of Y, N, T, or F for yes, no, true, or false. You can enter the character in either uppercase or lowercase. This field is particularly efficient for the computer to determine whether it should perform a task according to whether the answer is Y, N, T, or F. For example, is 2+3=5? Answer: T

Date A date is normally expressed as mm/dd/yy such as 03/21/94 for March 21, 1994. FoxPro allows you to use some other formats such as yy/mm/dd.

Memo This field accepts any printable text.

The field types and widths of the example database are shown in the following table. The widths of the fields are the best estimate of possible lengths of the fields.

	Field Name	Type	Width	Index	Field Description
1	*lastname*	C	24	Y	Last name of client
2	*morename*	C	24		Other names of client
3	*id_num*	C	4	Y	I.D. number of client
4	*jobtype*	C	3	Y	Occupational category
5	*title*	C	24		Position title
6	*employer*	C	36		Employer company name
7	*street*	C	36		Employer street address
8	*city*	C	24		City name of address
9	*state*	C	2	Y	State abbreviation
10	*zip*	C	10	Y	Zip code of address

11	*howmany*	N	2		No. of seminars attended
12	*lastdate*	D	8	Y	Date of last seminar
13	*notepad*	M	10		Memo field

INDEX Indexing makes search of information more efficient. When you ask for a field to be indexed, FoxPro sets up an index tag for the field which is used along with the database. FoxPro logically sorts the order of the records according to the values of the indexed field in either an ascending or descending order. For example, if the field is *state* and the values of this field in records 1,2,..5 are "MO," "CA," "WA," "MO," and "NC," then the index is something like "CA(2)," "MO(1)," "MO(4)," "NC(5)," and "WA(3)." Now if you ask FoxPro to pick "MO," it quickly picks records 1 and 4.

FoxPro lets you index as many fields as you want. But should you index every field? The answer depends on how often you want to use the index of a field for information retrieval. If you use a field often, it is a good idea to index it. Generally, a long field is not good for retrieval and need not be indexed. Some fields contain very diverse information and again are not good for retrieval. An example is the title field in the example database. Titles are long and cannot be grouped easily as the occupational categories.

In the example database, the fields to be indexed are marked with a "Y" (for yes) under the Index column in the foregoing table.

CREATING A DATABASE STRUCTURE

You can start creating a FoxPro database structure for the example database, *seminar.dbf.* FoxPro identifies a database file with a file extension *.dbf.* Here are the steps to follow.

1. Click on the File menu and select the **New** option.
2. Accept Database (the radio button) in the dialog by clicking **OK** or pressing **Ctrl+Enter**.
3. A dialog appears. See the following figure.

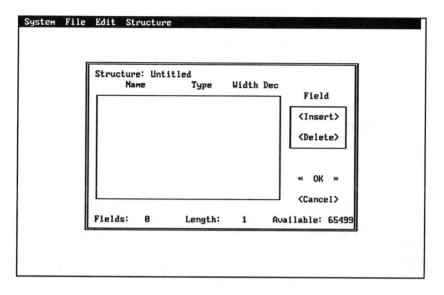

4. Type the first field name **lastname**.

5. Notice that a double-headed arrow appears as soon as you have typed **l** and FoxPro suggests a character field type and a field width of 10.

TIP: If you accidentally type a numeral, say, "3," for the first letter of a field name, an error message appears. Press Backspace to remove the error.

6. Press **Tab** twice to accept the field type. The cursor moves to the Width column.

7. Type **24**. FoxPro erases 10 and the column now reads 24.

8. Press **Tab**. The cursor is now in the second field.

9. Repeat steps 4 through 8 for field 2 until the end of field 10, using the field names and widths specified on the previous pages. After entering the "zip" field, the cursor should be at the beginning of field 11.

10. Type **howmany**. Now FoxPro again suggests a character field.

11. Select **Numeric**, using one of the following procedures.

   a. Procedure 1:

      (1) Click on the **Type** popup and drag the mouse to highlight Numeric and release the button.

b. Procedure 2:

(1) Press **Spacebar** to open the popup. See the following figure.

(2) Press **Down Arrow** to highlight Numeric.

(3) Press **Spacebar** to select and close the popup.

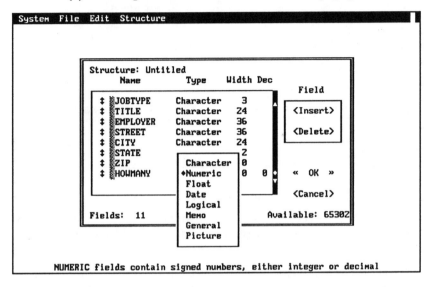

TIP: A faster way to make the selection is to type **N** (for Numeric).

12. Press **Tab** to move the cursor to the Width column.

13. Type **2** and press **Tab**. FoxPro suggests zero for the Dec (decimal) column. Accept this and do nothing.

14. Press **Tab** to move the cursor to field 12.

15. Type **lastdate**. Press **Tab**.

16. Type **D** for Date. The field width automatically changes to 8 and the cursor moves to the next field.

17. Type **notepad** and press **Tab**.

18. Type **M** for memo. You can ignore the field width because a memo field can be of any length.

Now you have completed typing all the fields. Proofread the typing. If you need to make a correction, click on the target column or press Tab or Shift+Tab to move the cursor there. Then use the Left or Right Arrow key to move the cursor to the target character, type the correction, and use the Backspace or Del key to delete any extra character.

INDEXING   The next task is to index fields 1, 3, 4, 9, 10, and 12. Notice the shaded vertical bar to the left of each field name. It is the index indicator. Here are the steps to do indexing.

1.   a.   With the mouse:

   (1) Drag the Thumb upward or downward until *lastname* is visible.

   b.   With the keyboard:

   (1) Press **Tab** to move the cursor into the scrollable list.

   (2) Press **Up** or **Down Arrow** until *lastname* is highlighted.

2. Double-click on the shaded bar of *lastname* or press **Shift+Tab** to move the cursor there and then press **Spacebar**.

3. Notice that an up arrow appears, showing the index is in the ascending order.

4. Double-click on the shaded bar or press **Spacebar** once more and the arrow turns downward showing the index is descending.

5. Double-click on the shaded bar or press **Spacebar** one more time and there is no index.

6. Bring back the ascending index by double-clicking on the shaded bar or pressing **Spacebar** again.

7. Index the fields *id_num, jobtype, state, zip,* and *lastdate*: Double-click on the shaded bar of each field or press **Down Arrow** to the shaded bar of each field and press **Spacebar**.

SAVING THE DATABASE FILE   Here are the steps to tell FoxPro that the database structure is completed, and it can be saved.

1. Click on **OK** or press **Ctrl+Enter**. A dialog appears. See the following figure.

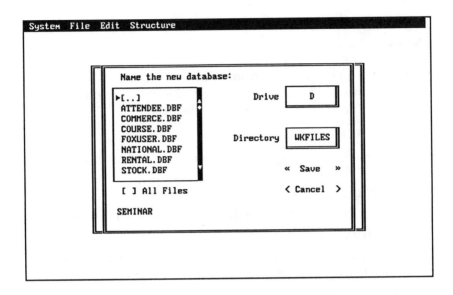

2. Notice that your current drive is D: and your current directory is WKFILES. This is exactly what you want. No change is necessary.

3. Type **SEMINAR** in the text area of the dialog.

4. Click on **Save** or press **Ctrl+Enter** to save the file. FoxPro asks you if you want to enter data now. Type **N** to stop for a moment.

ADDING (APPENDING) DATA RECORDS

FoxPro considers the file empty until at least one record is stored in it. You can start adding records to the file. FoxPro uses the term APPEND rather than ADD. You use this option to add records. You need not open the file first because the file remains open after the last exercise.

There are two screen display modes for you to choose from: the Change mode and the Browse mode. You can try both. You can use the data shown in the following table to build 15 records.

Record #1 Motti; Mark K.; 1630; MGM; Policy Advisor; Pan American Investment Co. Inc.; 1812 White Rose Blvd.; Jersey City; NJ; 07322; 1; 06/14/89.

Record #2 Lewis; Amy K.; 1715; ECO; Economist; Fragrance Paper Products Inc.; 141 Warren Road; Newark; NJ; 07045; 4; 02/18/92.

Record #3 Andrews; Lucy L.; 1726; ECO; Economic Advisor; Regional Savings Bank; 257 Admiral Street; Jersey City; NJ; 07333; 3; 02/18/92.

Record #4 Lobo; Frances P.; 1730; MGM; Management Consultant; Mohawk Mutual Funds Inc.; 159 Main Street; Jersey City; NJ; 07398; 2; 09/21/91.

Record #5 Davidson; Patrick J.; 1735; ACC; Chief Accountant; New Jersey Oil Co. Inc.; 123 Walnut Street; Newark; NJ; 07091; 2; 09/21/91.

Record #6 Bohm; Judy M.; 1758; ECO; Financial Analyst; Excel Printing Ink Co. Inc.; 298 Atlantic Avenue; Newark; NJ; 07280; 2; 09/21/91.

Record #7 Slater; Nancy P.; 1794; ECO; Economist; Pan American Investment Co. Inc.; 1812 White Rose Blvd.; Jersey City; NJ; 07322; 2; 02/18/92.

Record #8 Kelly; Rose L.; 1801; ECO; Economist; Simons Pharmaceutical Products Inc.; 268 Southam Road; Atlantic City; NJ; 07564; 3; 02/18/92.

Record #9 Chan; Joseph T.; 1821; MGM; Management Accountant; Synthetic Fibres Co. Inc; 100 Commerce Court; Newark; NJ; 07035; 2; 02/18/92.

Record #10 Lewandowski; Anthony F.; 1825; ACC; Senior Accountant; Synthetic Fibres Co. Inc.; 100 Commerce Court; Newark; NJ; 07035; 1; 02/18/92.

Record #11 Condi; Marion K.; 1854; ACC; Accountant; Confederation Chemical Co. Inc.; 876 San Diego Road; Jersey City; NJ; 07342; 3; 02/18/92.

Record #12 Rando; Cynthia L.; 1862; MGM; Financial Consultant; Superior Mutual Funds Inc.; 542 Locust Blvd.; Newark; NJ; 07095; 1; 11/25/91.

Record #13 Rankin; Susan T.; 1870; ACC; Account Manager; Superior Mutual Funds Inc.; 542 Locust Blvd.; Newark; NJ; 07095; 2; 11/25/91.

Record #14 Davis; John M.; 1886; ACC; Accountant; Pan American Investment Co. Inc.; 1812 White Rose Blvd.; Jersey City; NJ; 07322; 1; 11/25/91.

Record #15 Marks; Stephen M.; 1892; ECO; Economist; Regional Savings Bank; 257 Admiral Street; Jersey City; NJ; 07333; 1; 02/18/92.

USING THE CHANGE MODE

1. Select the Record menu and **Append** option. A data entry window appears. This window is in the Change mode. See the following figure.

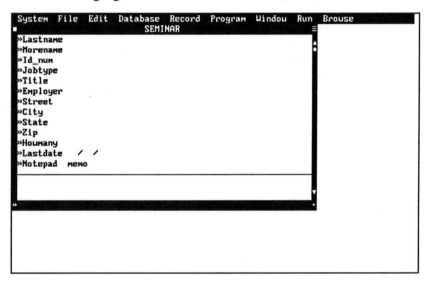

2. Notice that FoxPro has added a Browse menu to the menu bar.
3. Type **Motti** in the *lastname* field. Press **Tab**.
4. Type **Mark K.** in the *morename* field. Press **Tab**.
5. Type **1630** in the *id_num* field. This field is completely filled and the cursor jumps to the next field automatically.
6. Type **MGM** in the *jobtype* field. No Tab is needed.
7. Type **Policy Advisor** in the *title* field. Press **Tab**.
8. Type **Pan American Investment Co. Inc.** in the *employer* field. Press **Tab**.
9. Type **1812 White Rose Blvd.** in the *street* field. Press **Tab**.

10. Type **Jersey City** in the *city* field. Press **Tab**.

11. Type **NJ** in the *state* field. No Tab is needed.

12. Type **07322** in the *zip* field. Press **Tab**.

13. Type **1** in the *howmany* field. Press **Tab**.

14. Type **061489** in the *lastdate* field. No Tab is needed.

15. Press **Tab** to skip over the memo field to the next record.

16. Repeat steps 3 through 15 to enter data for records 2 to 8 until the memo field of record 8.

Entering Text in the Memo Field

1. Open the memo field of record 8: Double-click on the memo field or press **Tab** to move the cursor to this field and then press **Ctrl+PgDn**. The memo editing window appears. See the following figure.

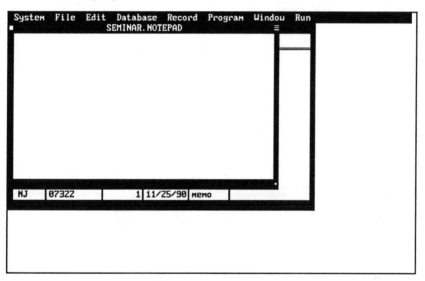

2. Notice that the window title at the top of the window is SEMINAR.NOTEPAD. The dot indicates that *notepad* is a field of SEMINAR.DBF.

3. Type the following text for this field in the window.

    Client interested in freelance distributorship of seminar video and audio cassettes. Has business associates in Britain, Western

> **Europe and the Far East. Annual business volume expected to be $300,000.**

TIP: Use the Del, Backspace, or arrow keys to correct errors if necessary. Notice that you can change the size of the editing window if you want.

Notice that FoxPro wraps the words around for you as the text reaches the end of a line. Press **Enter** only between paragraphs.

4. Click on the Close box or select the File menu and **Close** option to close the editing window.

TIP: You can discard what you have typed in a memo field by pressing Esc. The text is not saved and the editing window closes.

5. Notice that the word "memo" in the *notepad* field has changed to "Memo," indicating that this field is not empty.

USING THE BROWSE MODE

You may want to try the Browse mode now. But before you do that, take a look at the Change mode carefully. The Change mode displays the fields in a vertical column. Its focus is on an individual record. That is why this mode is placed in the Record menu. Compare this format with the Browse format you are going to see.

Here are the steps to follow.

1. Select the Browse menu and **Browse** option. The Browse window appears. See the following figure.

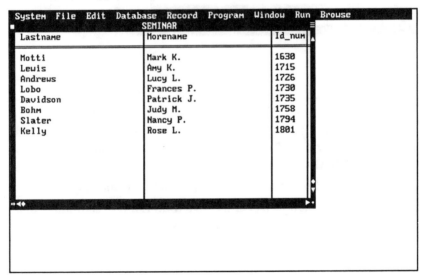

Lastname	Morename	Id_num
Motti	Mark K.	1630
Lewis	Amy K.	1715
Andrews	Lucy L.	1726
Lobo	Frances P.	1730
Davidson	Patrick J.	1735
Bohm	Judy M.	1758
Slater	Nancy P.	1794
Kelly	Rose L.	1801

System File Edit Database Record Program Window Run Browse
SEMINAR

2. Notice the Browse format. The field names have now become the column headings of the window. You can see several records at a time, but the screen is not wide enough to show all the fields.

3. Click on the Zoom control button or press **Ctrl+F10** to enlarge the window.

4. Scroll the window horizontally: Press **Tab** or drag the Thumb on the bottom scroll bar to the right to see the other fields.

5. Click on the *lastname* field of the empty record following record 8 and type **Chan**. Press **Tab**.

6. Type the remaining records. Press **Tab** as necessary to move the cursor from one field to the next.

7. Close the data entry window when finished: Click on the Close box of the window or select the File menu and **Close** option. This step also saves your records.

CHANGING (EDITING) EXISTING DATA

The procedures for changing data in existing records are very similar to adding records as you just did. FoxPro uses the term CHANGE rather than EDIT. You can use the Database menu or the Record menu.

ACCESSING THROUGH THE DATABASE MENU

1. Select the Database menu and **Browse** option. The Browse window in the Browse mode appears.

2. Notice that FoxPro has added the Browse menu to the menu bar.

3. Change the address of "Condi" to "876 San Diego Street."

    a. Click on the Thumb and drag the mouse until the record of "Condi" is visible; or press **Down** or **Up Arrow** to move the cursor to this record.

    b. Click in front of the word "Road" of the *street* field of the "Condi" record, or press **Tab** to move the cursor to this field and then press **Left** or **Right Arrow** to move the cursor to the word "Road."

4. Type **Street** and press **Del** to delete Road. Press **Tab**.

5. Save the changes: Click on the Close box or select the File menu and **Close** option.

ACCESSING THROUGH RECORD MENU

1. Select the Record menu and **Change** option. The Browse window in the Change mode appears.
2. Move the cursor to the record of "Condi" if necessary, and make the change as you did with the Browse mode.
3. Save the changes: Click on the Close box or select the File menu and **Close** option.

DELETING A DATA RECORD

You can delete a record or records from a database. A "deleted" record is not actually erased from the file. FoxPro merely marks it for deletion. FoxPro ignores a marked record in performing its tasks, such as doing a query or printing a report. You can undelete a marked record anytime before you ask FoxPro to erase it. You can do this by recalling the record. A marked record is permanently erased when you ask FoxPro to PACK it. Note that you cannot pack a record if it is not marked.

Another way to delete records is to ZAP the records. ZAP deletes *all* records of a database, although the database structure remains unaffected. Also, you need not mark the records before they are zapped. Because of its drastic action, ZAP should be used very infrequently and very carefully.

Now try to delete records #2 and #4 from SEMINAR.DBF. Do not worry, you can recall them afterwards. Here are the steps to follow.

1. Select the Database menu and **Browse** option. The Browse window returns.
2. Move the cursor to record #2 (Lewis, Amy K.): Click on the Thumb of the Browse window and drag the mouse until this record is visible and then click on the record; or press **Down Arrow** to highlight this record.
3. Select the Browse menu and **Toggle Delete** option.
4. Notice that a dot appears at the left of the field name to confirm that the record is marked.
5. Repeat steps 2 and 3 to delete record #4 (Lobo, Frances P).

6. Notice that you can PACK the "deleted" records by selecting the Database menu and Pack option. Do not actually make the deletion if you do not want to re-enter the records.

7. Recall records #2 and #4 by repeating steps 2 and 3.

8. Notice that the dots on records #2 and #4 disappear.

TIP: You can quickly mark and unmark a record for deletion by clicking on the left edge of the record.

MODIFYING A DATABASE STRUCTURE

The need to modify a database structure should arise very infrequently. It is good practice to design a database structure before it is used and, in the design, consider all foreseeable situations. You should be aware that, when the structure of a database is changed, you may need to modify the existing data and the application programs which use the database. In these modifications, it is possible to miss something or mix up things. When these problems occur, you may have difficulty in retrieving information—some of the information may not be retrievable, some may be incorrectly retrieved, and so on.

For example, suppose the address field of a database originally includes the state abbreviation and the zip code. The required modification is to place the state and the zip code in two new fields separate from the address field. The two new fields are intended to help information retrieval focusing at the state and the zip code. Imagine how clumsy it will be to move the state and the zip code from the address field to the two new fields. The problem can be acute when the file is large. There may be another problem too. If an original application program is not modified to make use of these two new fields, the data contained in the two new fields cannot be retrieved. Can a letter without the state and the zip code be delivered?

As an exercise, however, you can insert a new field for the gender of the clients into SEMINAR.DBF before the *title* field. Use a logical field, and a T value (for True) represents female. An F value represents male. Here are the steps to follow.

1. Select the Database menu and **Setup** option. A dialog box appears. See the following figure.

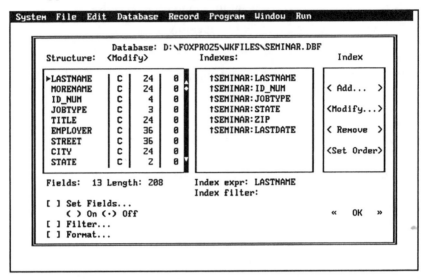

2. Select **Modify** near the top left corner of the box (not the one under "Indexes"). A Database Structure dialog appears which you saw before.
3. Move the cursor to the *title* field: Click on this field or press **Shift+Tab** to move the cursor there.
4. Select **Insert**.
5. Type **gender** in the new field provided and press **Tab**.
6. Type **L** (for logical). The width automatically reads "1."
7. Select **OK** to save the change.
8. Choose **Yes** when FoxPro asks you if you want to make the change permanent. FoxPro copies the existing records to this modified database.
9. Select **OK** to exit the Setup dialog.
10. Edit the 15 records to add data to the *gender* field.
    a. Select the Database menu and **Browse** option.
    b. Press **Tab** to move the cursor to the *gender* field of record #1. Type **F**.
    c. Repeat step 10b to enter data on the *gender* field of the remaining 14 records.

You have created a new database and practiced how to maintain it. As your database grows in size with more records, you want to be able to browse the file efficiently. Section 5 introduces you to useful features of the Browse window.

Section 5

BROWSING YOUR DATA

THE GOTO FUNCTION

If your database contains many records, it takes you a while to scroll to the target record with the arrow keys. Scrolling with the Thumb is faster. A more convenient way to reach a target record quickly is to use the GOTO function. Since there are only 15 records in SEMINAR.DBF, there is not much advantage to use the GOTO function. But you can try it for the sake of practice. Here are the steps to follow.

1. Select the Database menu and **Browse** option.
2. Select the Browse menu and **Goto** option. A dialog appears. See the following figure.

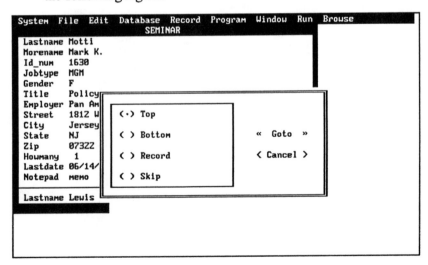

3. Click on **Record** or type **R**. The Record text area is highlighted.

4. Type **4** and press **Ctrl+Enter**.

5. Notice that the cursor has moved to the first field of record #4.

6. Repeat step 2 for the other three choices.

    a. Select **Bottom** and then select **Goto**. The cursor moves to the last record of the file.

    b. Select **Top** and then select **Goto**. The cursor moves to the top record of the file.

    c. Select **Skip**. The Skip text area appears highlighted.

    d. Type **3** and press **Ctrl+Enter** to skip three records.

    e. Notice that the cursor is now on the 4th record after skipping records 1, 2, and 3.

7. Try Cancel: Repeat step 2. Select **Top** and then select **Cancel**. FoxPro cancels your request.

THE BROWSE WINDOW

The Browse window has the typical features of the System window. You can move it, resize it, and scroll it. In addition, the Browse window has six other interesting features. You can:

- Split the window into two, like the following figure
- Change the active window from the left window to the right window and the other way around
- Link and unlink the split windows
- Have one window in the Browse mode and the other window in the Change mode, or both windows have the same mode
- Move a data field from one column to another
- Change the width of a field

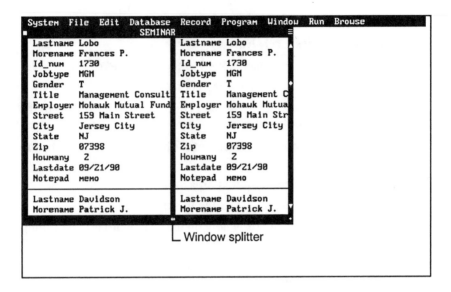

Using these features does not alter your database. What you see in the Browse window is actually a copy of your database and not the real original.

Why do we want to have this convenience? Here is an illustrative answer. Suppose you have many records in a database and you want to locate a record quickly and then look at the details of this record. You can set one of the windows to the Browse mode and the other to the Change mode. You make the window in the Browse mode active and scroll the data in it quickly to locate the target record. When it is found, you make the other window active and look at the details of the target record in this window.

You can use the active window to do data entry or data editing as you did with an unsplit Browse or Change window.

TO SPLIT THE WINDOW

1. With the mouse:

   a. Click on the window splitter at the bottom left corner of the window and drag the mouse to your right. You see a window emerging on the left side.

   b. Release the button when the windows are the sizes you want.

   c. Repeat steps 1a and 1b to close the windows, but drag the mouse to the left this time.

2. With the keyboard:

   a. Select the Browse menu and **Resize Partitions** option. The window splitter at the bottom left corner of the window blinks.

   b. Press the **Right Arrow** key until the two windows have the sizes you like. Press **Enter**. The window splitter stops blinking.

   c. Repeat steps 2a and 2b to close the windows, pressing the **Left Arrow** key this time.

TO SELECT ACTIVE WINDOW   One of the two split windows is active at a time. The cursor is in the active window and you can work with this window; for example, change data. Suppose the current active window is the right window and you want to activate the left window. Here is the step to follow.

1. Click on the left window (anywhere in the data area of the left window) or select the Browse menu and **Change Partition** option. The left window becomes the active window.

TO UNLINK THE SPLIT WINDOWS   The default is for the two windows to be linked. That is, when one window scrolls, say three records downward, the other window does likewise. The two windows can be unlinked. In the unlinked state, while you scroll the active window to bring records that are off the screen into view, those in the inactive window do not move.

You have to use the Browse menu to unlink the windows. Here are the steps to follow.

1. Select the Browse menu and **Link/Unlink Partitions** option. Notice that this is a toggle option. The prompt reads Unlink Partitions if your windows are currently linked, and Link if the windows are currently unlinked.

2. Reselect the **Link Partitions** option.

TO SWITCH BETWEEN BROWSE AND CHANGE MODES

1. Make the target window the active window.
2. Select the Browse menu and **Change** option. The active window changes to the Change mode.
3. Select the Browse menu and **Browse** option. The active window changes to the Browse mode.
4. Close the partitions when done.

TO MOVE THE POSITION OF A FIELD   In the Browse mode, the screen may not be wide enough to display all the fields of a record. Of course, you can use the Tab or Shift+Tab keys to scroll the screen to bring the undisplayed fields into view. This approach, however, can be tedious if you have a lot of browsing to do. FoxPro provides a handy solution to this problem. You can move the target fields to line up one after another, so you can see all of them in one screen. Here are the steps to follow.

1. With the mouse:
   a. Point to the field's name, not the data.
   b. Press the button and drag the mouse left or right to the desired position.
   c. Release the button when the field is where you desire.
   d. Notice that you can move a field in a split window. When you move a field in one window, the same field moves to the corresponding position in the other window.
2. With the keyboard:
   a. Press **Tab** or **Shift+Tab** to move the cursor to the target field.
   b. Select the Browse menu and **Move Field** option.
   c. Press **Left** or **Right Arrow** to move the target field to the desired position and then press **Enter**.

TO CHANGE THE FIELD WIDTH   You can increase or decrease the width of a field.

1. With the mouse:
   a. Click on the vertical grid line on the right-hand side of the target field name and drag the mouse left or right until the field size is what you like.

   b. Release the button.

2. With the keyboard:

   a. Press **Tab** or **Shift+Tab** to move the cursor to the target field name.

   b. Select the Browse menu and **Size Field** option.

   c. Press **Left** or **Right Arrow** to change the size of the field until you like it. Press **Enter**.

3. Press **Esc** to close the Browse window when you are done with browsing.

You have created your own database and used it successfully. You are ready for the next leg of your journey in FoxPro to retrieve data from your database.

Section 6

RQBE: ORDERING AND GROUPING DATA

INTRODUCTION

The FoxPro power tool, RQBE, is able to retrieve complex information from a single database and multiple databases. *RQBE* stands for Relational Query By Example which, in turn, needs some explanation.

Relational means joining multiple databases used in an information retrieval process according to some relationship specified by the user. For example, you can join the database SEMINAR.DBF with two other databases, ATTENDEE.DBF and COURSE.DBF, which are on the diskette supplied with this book. The relationship can be changed by the user from one information retrieval exercise to another. The flexibility of change depends on the design and contents of the databases.

Query is used to retrieve certain information from a database or databases required for a specific purpose. Other information in the databases not required for the specific purpose is not retrieved, so no irrelevant information will be presented in the query report. This ability to retrieve purpose-specific information is the single most important reason for going for database management.

By Example is to describe, by an example or examples, what specific information should be retrieved. You tell RQBE your requirements by "an example." An example may be something like "Count the number of seminar attendees who belong to the accountant occupational group."

Retrieving information from a database does not alter any data in the database being used. What RQBE does is copy the relevant information from the database and present the copied information to the user. Therefore, a database can be used for queries repeatedly and one query can be different from another. You can save a query for repeated uses if you want. Let us begin to run RQBE.

THE RQBE WINDOW

Look at the features of the RQBE window which is shown in the following figure.

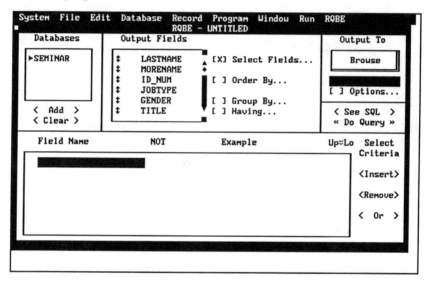

- The name of the query file, RQBE - UNTITLED, appears in the top border of the window.
- The Close box is located at the top left corner of the window.
- The database in use is displayed in the Databases list.
- All the data fields of the database in use, SEMINAR.DBF, are included in the Output Fields list. This is the initial default setting. You can modify this list to include only those fields that you want to include in a query report.
- The check boxes are for you to organize the presentation of your query results.

- The big rectangular box in the lower part of the RQBE window is the Selection Criteria box. You specify your criteria of a query in this place.

- The See SQL push button enables you to see the SQL commands used in doing a query. *SQL* stands for *Structured Query Language*. It is a very powerful computer language used for doing queries. If you want to learn SQL in the future, you may want to select See SQL and view the commands. You need not learn SQL in using RQBE.

- The Output To popup is for you to specify where the query results should be sent: To the Browse window, to printer, and so forth.

- Notice the hot keys; for example, F is the hot key for the Select Fields check box.

CREATING A QUERY

This exercise is to prepare a list of all seminar attendees from the SEMINAR.DBF database. The list should include only the following data fields: *lastname, id_num, employer, jobtype, howmany,* and *lastdate.*

Here are the steps to follow.

1. Select the File menu and **New** option.
2. Select **Query** from the dialog and then select **OK**. The RQBE window appears.
3. Choose **Select Fields**. A dialog appears. See the following figure.

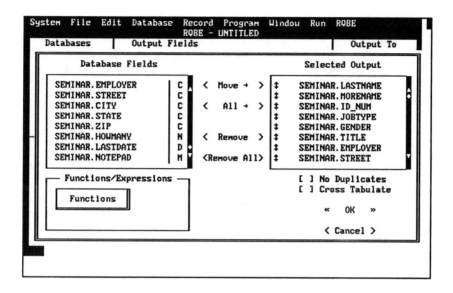

Notice that all the fields in the Database Fields list are dimmed since FoxPro has preselected all of them for output.

4. Remove all the data fields from the Selected Output list: Click on **Remove All** or type **L**.

5. Move *seminar.lastname* from the Database Fields list to the Selected Output list.

   a. With the mouse:

      (1) Double-click on *seminar.lastname* in the Database Fields list.

      (2) Notice that this field name now appears in the Selected Output list and the same name in the Database Fields list becomes dimmed.

   b. With the keyboard:

      (1) Press **Tab** to move the cursor to the Database Fields list.

      (2) Press **Down Arrow** to highlight *seminar.lastname*.

      (3) Press **Spacebar** twice in rapid succession.

      (4) Notice that the field name now appears in the Selected Output list and the same name in the Database Fields list becomes dimmed.

TIP: Step 5 is the general procedure used for moving a data field from one list to another in RQBE, regardless of what the list is. You use the same procedure for moving a field in the reverse direction, for example, from the Selected Output list back to the Database Fields list. In the reverse move, the origin list is the Selected Output list and the destination list is the Database Fields list.

6. Move *seminar.id_num*, *seminar.employer*, *seminar.jobtype*, *seminar.howmany*, and *seminar.lastdate* to the Selected Output list.

7. Reposition *seminar.id_num* to the top of the Selected Output list.

  a. With the mouse:

   (1) Click on the double-headed arrow of *seminar.id_num*, drag the field to the top of the list, then release the button.

  b. With the keyboard:

   (1) Press **Tab** to move the cursor to this list.

   (2) Press **Down Arrow** to reach the desired field.

   (3) Press **Ctrl+PgUp** to move this field to the top of the list.

TIP: Step 7 is the general procedure for repositioning a data field in a list where the data field has a double-headed arrow.

8. Select **OK** to return to the RQBE window.

9. Select **Do Query**. The query results appear in a Query window. See the following figure.

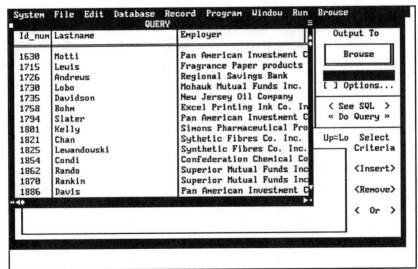

Notice that you can scroll the window and change its size. You can also move and resize the fields as you did with the Browse window.

10. Press **Esc** to close the Query window when done. Leave the RQBE window open for the next exercise.

ORDER BY

In this exercise, you want to arrange the names of the attendees according to *jobtype* in descending order and within each value of *jobtype*, according to the last names of the attendees in alphabetical order.

Beware that RQBE arranges the output data in the order of field selection. Therefore, you should select *jobtype* first and *lastname* second.

Here are the steps to follow.

1. Choose **Select Fields**. Remove *seminar.employer* from the Selected Output list.

2. Select **OK** to return to the RQBE window.

3. Select **Order By**. The RQBE Order By dialog appears. See the following figure.

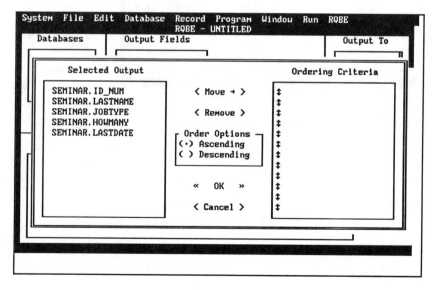

4. Select **Descending**.

5. Move *seminar.jobtype* to the Ordering Criteria list.

6. Select **Ascending** and then move *seminar.lastname* to the Ordering Criteria list.

7. Select **OK** to return to the RQBE window.

TIP: You cannot use *lastname* and *id_num* for ordering data in the same query because the order of these two fields cannot be compatible with each other.

8. Notice that in the Output Fields list, *jobtype* is marked with a numeral "1" and a down arrow; and *lastname* is marked with a numeral "2" and an up arrow. These marks indicate the sequence and descending/ascending order of the ordering criteria.

9. Select **Do Query**. Your results should look like the following figure.

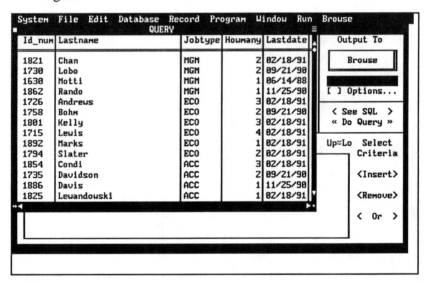

10. Press **Esc** to close the Query window when done.

11. Select the File menu and **Save As** option.

12. Type SECT6_1 in the highlighted text area. Press **Ctrl+Enter** to save the file.

How much did Order By improve the presentation quality of the query results?

GROUP BY

In this exercise, you ask RQBE to calculate the following statistics of each city: the number of attendees, the total number of seminars attended by all the clients, the maximum number of seminars attended by a client, and the average number of seminars attended per client. When you ask RQBE to calculate these statistics for each city, you use the Group By option to group (the data) by the *city* data field.

The mathematical functions used in this exercise are:

- COUNT(*): To count the number of selected records. This is equivalent to counting the number of attendees.
- SUM(*seminar.howmany*): To calculate the sum of seminars attended by all the clients.
- MAX(*seminar.howmany*): To determine the highest number of seminars attended by a client.
- AVG(*seminar.howmany*): To calculate the average number of seminars attended per client.

Here are the steps to follow.

1. Press **Esc** to close the current RQBE window.
2. Select the File menu and **New** option.
3. Select **Query** and **OK**. FoxPro presents the Open dialog.
4. Select SEMINAR.DBF and **Open**. A new RQBE window appears.
5. Choose **Select Fields**.
6. Remove all fields from the default Selected Output list.
7. Move *seminar.city* to the Selected Output list.
8. Select the COUNT(*) function.
   a. With the mouse:
      (1) Click on the **Functions/Expressions** popup to display the list of functions. The cursor rests on the first function, COUNT( ). Click on COUNT. A companion list of data fields also appears. See the following figure.

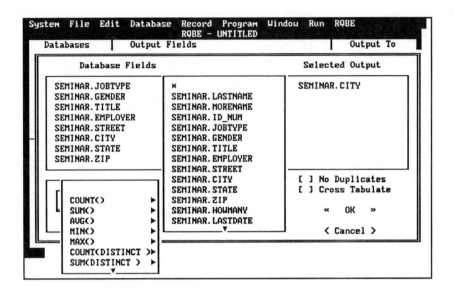

(2) Click on * on the companion list. The popup and the companion list disappear.

(3) Notice that COUNT(*) appears in the text area below the Functions popup.

(4) Click on **Move**. COUNT(*) now appears in the Selected Output list.

b. With the keyboard:

(1) Press **Tab** to move the cursor to the Functions popup.

(2) Press **Spacebar** to display the list of functions.

(3) Press **Spacebar** to accept COUNT. A list of data fields appears.

(4) Press **Enter** to accept *.

(5) Type **M** to move the function to the Selected Output list.

9. Repeat step 8 to select and move SUM(*seminar.howmany*), MAX(*seminar.howmany*), and AVG(*seminar.howmany*) to the Selected Output list. Drag the mouse or press **Down Arrow** as necessary to select the desired function and the desired data field.

10. Select **OK** to return to the RQBE window.

11. Select **Group By**. A dialog appears. See the following figure.

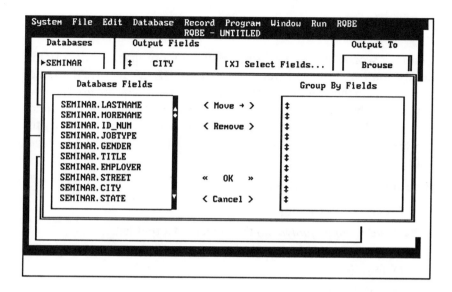

12. Move *seminar.city* to the Group By Fields list. Select **OK**.

13. Select **Do Query**.

14. Enlarge the Query window and resize the fields to bring all fields into one screen. See the following figure.

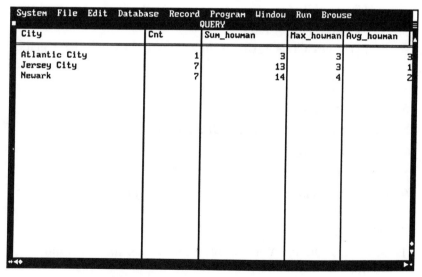

15. Check the results manually.

16. Press **Esc** to close the Query window when done.

NESTED GROUPING

You may wonder if you can group data by more than one data field. Surely you can. In this exercise, you ask RQBE to calculate the same statistics as in the previous exercise. However, the data are grouped by *city*, and within each city, grouped by *jobtype*. Grouping one data field within another is called *nested grouping*. You add more complexity to this exercise by ordering the results by *city* alphabetically and *jobtype* in descending order.

Here are the steps to follow.

1. Choose **Select Fields**.
2. Move *seminar.jobtype* to the Selected Output list.
3. Position *seminar.jobtype* below *seminar.city* on the Selected Output list.
   a. With the mouse:
      (1) Click on the double-headed arrow on the left side of *seminar.jobtype* and drag it up to the next place below *seminar.city*.
   b. With the keyboard:
      (1) Press **Tab** to move the cursor to *seminar.jobtype* on the Selected Output list.
      (2) Press **Ctrl+PgUp** to move this field to the next place below *seminar.city*.
4. Select **OK**.
5. Select **Group By**.
6. Move *seminar.jobtype* to the Group By Fields list and select **OK**.
7. Select **Order By**.
8. Move *seminar.city* to the Ordering Criteria list.
9. Select **Descending**. Move *seminar.jobtype* to the Ordering Criteria list.
10. Select **OK**.
11. Select **Do Query**. Your results should look like the following figure.

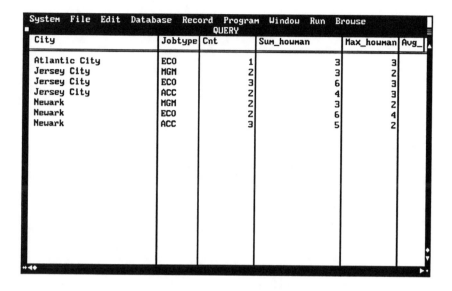

12. Press **Esc** to close the Query window.

13. Select the File menu and **Save As** option.

14. Type **SECT6_2** in the highlighted text area. Press **Ctrl+Enter** to save the file.

15. Press **Esc** to close the RQBE window.

In Section 6, you have learned how to use the Fields, Order By, Group By, nested grouping, mathematical functions, and Do Query. How do you like the RQBE's capabilities so far? Is RQBE easy to learn and use? In the next section, you begin to use RQBE to select data records based on your specific selection criteria.

RQBE: POWERFUL DATA RETRIEVAL

THE USE OF QUERIES

The queries done in Section 6 retrieved all records of SEMINAR.DBF. On various occasions, however, you may want to include only certain records of the database in a query for a certain purpose. For example, you may want to create a list of attendees who are accountants so the seminar firm may mail course information to this group of clients. When you retrieve information in this selective manner, you are truly doing a query. From this illustration, you can see that queries are useful in many business applications.

IMPORTANCE OF SELECTING CORRECT CRITERIA

It is very important to have correct selection criteria for a query. Improper selection of criteria impairs the quality of query results. For example, suppose the seminar firm wants to send a brochure of a new course entitled *How to Project Your Professional Image* designed exclusively for female accountants. In this case, it will be improper to use *jobtype* alone as the selection criterion in creating a client list. The *gender* field must be used also. If the *gender* field is not used, the seminar firm will unintentionally send the brochure to male accountants also. The male accountants who receive the brochures may wonder about the business competence of the seminar firm.

COMPOSING A QUERY

It is useful to compose a query in plain language first and then translate the query into selection criteria in the language that RQBE can understand.

Consider this example. The seminar firm wants a list of clients who are accountants and who live in zip code areas between "07000" and "07299." The word *and* linking the fields *jobtype* and *zip* is very important. This word requires that for a record to be selected, it must satisfy both criteria, not just one of them. You can imagine the information retrieval process mentally. It is a two-step process. In the first step, select all records with *jobtype* equal to "ACC." In the second step, examine each of the records selected in step 1 and select only those with *zip* between "07000" and "07299."

RQBE TERMINOLOGY

The following figure shows a list of RQBE comparators used in query. You can notice that this list is contained in a popup in the Selection Criteria box. RQBE selects a record if the value of the data field of the record matches the value you have defined in your selection criteria. The comparison is based on the comparator or comparators you have selected. The comparison result is *true* if there is a match, and *false* if not.

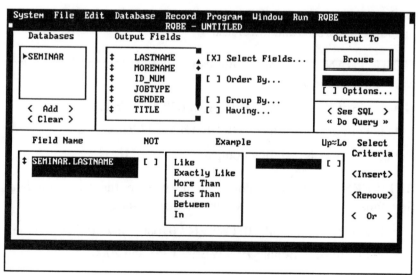

Before you do query exercises with RQBE, look at the following examples which help you understand how the comparators work.

LIKE This comparator is used for comparison of two data values of the same type, for example, character with character or numeric with numeric.

- Is *jobtype* of "Condi" LIKE "ACC"? True.
- Is *jobtype* of "Condi" LIKE "ECO"? False.
- Is *jobtype* of "Condi" NOT LIKE "ECO"? True.
- Is *lastname* of "Lewandowski" LIKE "Lew"? True.
- Is *lastname* of "Lewandowski" LIKE "LEW"? False.

Notice that LIKE accepts a truncated string, "Lew," in the query input. Notice also that although LIKE considers "Lewandowski" a good match with "Lew," it does not do so with "LEW" because of the difference in uppercase and lowercase.

EXACTLY LIKE This comparator demands a more strict match than does LIKE.

- Is *jobtype* of "Condi" EXACTLY LIKE "ACC"? True.
- Is *jobtype* of "Condi" EXACTLY LIKE "Acc"? False.
- Is *lastname* of "Lewandowski" EXACTLY LIKE "Lew"? False.

Notice that EXACTLY LIKE requires a character-by-character match, including uppercase and lowercase.

MORE THAN This comparator can be used for comparison of two data values of the same type.

- Is *zip* of "Chan" MORE THAN "07000"? True.
- Is *howmany* of "Chan" MORE THAN 4? False.

Notice that there is a similar comparator LESS THAN.

BETWEEN This comparator evaluates whether the value of a data field falls within the range of values defined in the query input.

- Is *zip* of "Davidson" BETWEEN "07000" and "07299"? True.
- Is *id_num* of "Bohm" BETWEEN 1758 and 2000? True.

IN This comparator evaluates whether the value of a data field matches one of the values defined in the query input.

- Is *city* of "Slater" IN "Jersey City,Newark"? True.
- Is *city* of "Slater" IN "Newark,Atlantic City"? False.

Now that you understand the purposes and effects of the comparators, you may want to do the exercises which follow. While you learn new techniques in these exercises, you still need to use the techniques for moving and ordering data fields. Revisit Section 6 if necessary to review these techniques.

USING LIKE/EXACTLY LIKE COMPARATORS

This exercise is to prepare a list of seminar attendees from SEMINAR.DBF who are accountants. You can make use of the query file SECT6_1.QPR prepared in Section 6.

Here are the steps to follow.

1. Select the File menu and **Open** option. The Open dialog appears.
2. Select **Query** from the Type popup.
3. Select SECT6_1.QPR: Double-click on this file or press **Down Arrow** to highlight this file and select **Open**. The RQBE-Sect6_1 window opens.
4. Select **Order By**. Remove ordering criterion *seminar.jobtype* by double-clicking on it. Select **OK**.
5. Select *jobtype* as a selection criterion.
   a. With the mouse:
      (1) Click on the text box directly below Field Name, drag the mouse to select *seminar.jobtype* from the popup, then release the button.
   b. With the keyboard:
      (1) Press **Tab** to highlight the input area in the text box below Field Name.
      (2) Press **Spacebar** to open the popup.
      (3) Press **Down Arrow** to highlight *seminar.jobtype*.
      (4) Press **Spacebar** to select this field.
6. Notice that RQBE has selected the Like comparator by default.

7. Click on the Example text area or press **Tab** to move the cursor to this area. Type **ACC**.

8. Select **Do Query**. Your results should look like the following figure.

System	File	Edit	Database	Record	Program	Window	Run	Browse

QUERY

Id_num	Lastname	Jobtype	Howmany	Lastdate
1854	Condi	ACC	3	02/18/91
1735	Davidson	ACC	2	09/21/90
1886	Davis	ACC	1	11/25/90
1825	Lewandowski	ACC	1	02/18/91
1870	Rankin	ACC	2	11/25/90

9. Press **Esc** to close the Query window when you are done.

10. Select the File menu and **Save As** option.

11. Type **SECT7_1** in the text area and press **Ctrl+Enter** to save the file.

You can use a partial string of characters as the Example when using the Like comparator. Try the following exercise.

1. Remove the existing selection criteria Field Name line.

   a. Click on *Seminar.jobtype* or press **Tab** to highlight this line.

   b. Click on **Remove** or type **R**. The line disappears.

2. Select *seminar.lastname* for the Field Name. RQBE again has selected the Like comparator by default.

3. Type **Lew** in the Example text area.

4. Select **Do Query**. You should get two records: "Lewandowski" and "Lewis."

5. Press **Esc** to close the Query window.

Finally, try the Exactly Like comparator.

1. Select the Exactly Like comparator.

   a. With the mouse:

      (1) Click on the **Comparator** popup, drag the mouse to select **Exactly Like**, then release the button.

   b. With the keyboard:

      (1) Press **Tab** to highlight this popup area.

      (2) Press **Spacebar** to open the popup.

      (3) Press **Down Arrow** to highlight the Exactly Like comparator.

      (4) Press **Spacebar** to select this comparator.

      (5) Compare the similarity of making a selection from popups.

2. Leave "Lew" in the Example text area.

3. Select **Do Query**. You should get no records.

4. Press **Esc** to close the Query window.

USING OR/IN COMPARATORS

In this exercise, select clients who live in either Jersey City or Newark. Disregard their occupations.

1. Remove the existing selection criteria line.

2. Choose **Select Fields**.

3. Move *seminar.city* to the Selected Output list. Move it to the top of the list by dragging its double-headed arrow button or by highlighting this field and then pressing **Ctrl+PgUp**.

4. Select **OK**.

5. Select **Order By**. Move *seminar.city* to the Ordering Criteria list.

6. Move *seminar.city* in the Ordering Criteria list to the top of this list. Select **OK**.

7. Select *seminar.city* as Field Name in the Selection Criteria box.

8. Accept the default Like comparator and do nothing.

9. Type **Jersey City** in the Example text area.

10. Select the Or comparator: Click on **Or** or type **O**.

11. Notice that OR appears as shown in the following figure.

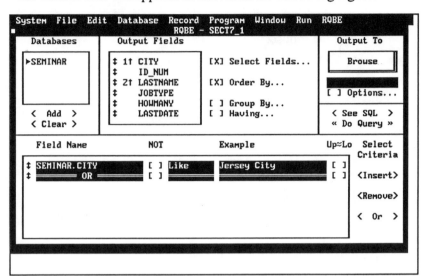

12. Select *seminar.city* as Field Name in the third criteria line. Accept the default Like comparator.

13. Type **Newark** in the Example text area for the second *seminar.city*.

14. Select **Do Query**. Your results should include all clients except Kelly, who lives in Atlantic City.

15. Press **Esc** to close the Query window.

You can accomplish the previous query in a simpler way by using the In comparator. Try the following exercise.

1. Remove the third selection criteria line.

2. Remove the OR selection criteria line in the same way as step 1.

3. Change the Like comparator in the first selection criteria line to the In comparator.

4. Move the cursor to the space immediately after "y" of "City" in the Example text area. Type ,**Newark**. Be sure to include the comma between the two city names.

5. Select **Do Query**. Your results should be the same as the previous one using the Or comparator.

6. Press **Esc** to close the Query Browse window.

7. Select the File menu and **Save As** option. Type **SECT7_2** in the text area and press **Ctrl+Enter** to save the file.

USING BETWEEN/NOT COMPARATORS

This exercise is to prepare a list of clients who do not live in Atlantic City (too far away from the seminar firm) and who last attended a seminar in either 1991 or 1992. Arrange the query results according to the city names and within each city name, according to the dates of seminars in descending order.

1. Select **Order By**. Remove *seminar.lastname* from the Ordering Criteria list.

2. Select **Descending** option and move *seminar.lastdate* to the Ordering Criteria list. Make sure seminar.city is at the top of the Ordering Criteria list and designated for Ascending order (with an "up" arrow to the left).

3. Select **OK**.

4. Select NOT in the first selection criteria line: Click on the check box below NOT in the Selection Criteria area.

5. Move the cursor to the Example text area. Type **Atlantic City**. Use **Del** to delete the extra text.

6. Select *seminar.lastdate* as the Field Name for the second selection criteria line.

7. Select the **Between** comparator.

8. Type **01/01/91,12/31/92** in the Example text area.

9. Select **Do Query**. Your results should look like the following figure.

```
System  File  Edit  Database  Record  Program  Window  Run  Browse
                                   QUERY
 City                      Id_num Lastname          Jobtype Howmany Las
 Jersey City               1726   Andreus           ECO          3  02/1
 Jersey City               1794   Slater            ECO          2  02/1
 Jersey City               1854   Condi             ACC          3  02/1
 Jersey City               1892   Marks             ECO          1  02/1
 Newark                    1715   Lewis             ECO          4  02/1
 Newark                    1821   Chan              MGM          2  02/1
 Newark                    1825   Lewandowski       ACC          1  02/1
```

10. Notice that there is no observable indication of how the first and second selection criteria lines are related. RQBE assumes that all selection criteria lines are connected by an And comparator unless you explicitly specify the Or comparator.

11. Press **Esc** to close the Query window.

12. Select the File menu and **Save As** option. Type **SECT7_3** in the text area and press **Ctrl+Enter** to save the file.

    Notice that you can use More Than 12/31/90 and Less Than 01/01/93 together to replace the Between comparator. However, the Between comparator is more efficient in this example.

13. Press **Esc** to close the RQBE window.

In Sections 6 and 7, you have learned how to use the powerful RQBE: to select output fields, to order and group the fields, and to use selection criteria. You may want to leave RQBE for now so you can learn how to prepare printed reports on your query results. Let us run the Report Writer in Section 8.

Section 8

REPORTING MADE EASY

INTRODUCTION

Printed reports are often required in database management, for example, invoices, employee annual income statements, or price catalogs. Instructing a computer to print a report is a very tedious task, but FoxPro's Report Writer makes the task simple for you. The Report Writer does the chores on your behalf. It can handle database information, work with RQBE, and perform calculations. It can also improve the quality of your report by means of its word processing capabilities.

When you prepare a report using the Report Writer, you actually design a layout of your report on the Report Layout window. When you finish the design of your report layout, you ask the Report Writer to print your report using your report layout. You can preview your report before you actually print it, so you can modify your report layout if necessary before printing. You can save a report layout for repeated uses.

REPORT LAYOUT WINDOW

Let us bring forward a report layout from the diskette supplied with this book to illustrate our discussions of the Report Layout window. Here are the steps to follow.

1. Select the File menu and **Open** option.

2. Select **Report** from the Type popup.

3. Select STOCK.FRX from the File Name list and then select **Open**. STOCK.FRX appears. See the following figure.

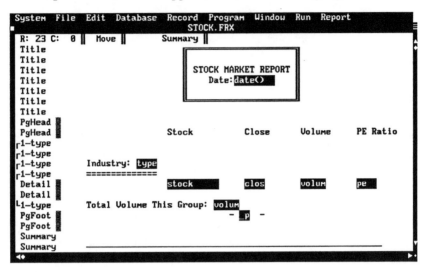

4. Drag the Thumb of the report window downward or press **Down Arrow** if necessary to see more of it.

The following describes the features of the Report Layout window shown in the figure.

THE REPORT LAYOUT WINDOW This window has many typical features of FoxPro's System window. Observe the title STOCK.FRX in the top border, the Close box at the top left corner of the window, and so forth.

THE BANDS Each report layout is organized into bands. Each band performs a specific function. There are seven bands in this illustration: Title, Page Header, Group Header (the lines titled "1-type" above "Detail"), Detail, Group Footer (the line titled "1-type" below "Detail"), Page Footer, and Summary. Drag the Thumb downward to see the hidden part of the window. The blank area to the right of each band title is for you to design your report layout. The height of this area can be changed. You can try it in a moment.

THE TITLE BAND You can use this band for such purposes as a report title page, an executive summary, or a description of selection criteria of the query being reported on. The Title band is printed once only at the beginning of a report.

THE SUMMARY BAND   It is similar to the Title band, but printed at the end of a report. In this illustration, it is used to report the day's total volume and value of the stocks traded.

THE PAGE HEADER BAND   It can be used for a page header such as "Reporting Made Easy" at the top of a page of this section of the book. In this illustration, it is used for the column headings "Stock," "Close," "Volume," and "PE Ratio" corresponding to the database fields. The Page Header is printed at the top of every page.

THE PAGE FOOTER BAND   It is similar to the Page Header, but printed at the foot of a page. In this illustration, it is used for page numbering.

THE DETAIL BAND   It is the space for reporting details of individual database records. In this illustration, this band consists of two lines. One line contains four data fields: *stock, close, volume,* and *pe.* The other line is blank to improve readability. Notice that the color shading of the fields is different from that of the text (field headings).

Although there is only one line for the data fields, the Detail band will stretch when the report is being printed. It will contain all the records selected for the report.

THE GROUP HEADER BAND   In this illustration, the stocks are grouped by the types of industries: "AUTO," "BANK," "FOOD," and "UTIL." Whenever the type changes as database records are turned during printing, this Group Header will be printed to indicate the new stock type.

THE GROUP FOOTER BAND   This is the area for reporting the summary of each group. In this illustration, it reports the total volume of each stock type traded.

The default Report Layout window shows three bands only: Page Header, Detail, and Page Footer. The other bands are added optionally according to the reporting needs. Although the Report Writer provides the Page Header and Page Footer bands by default, you can leave them blank if you want.

Let us have a quick look, or preview, of the real report of this layout.

PREVIEW

Here are the steps to preview the layout.

1. Select the Report menu and **Page Preview** option. The real report appears. It is no longer the report layout. See the following figure.

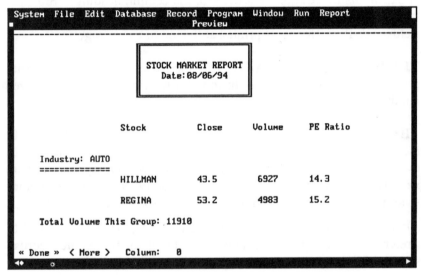

2. Notice that the data field names are now replaced with the actual values of the fields of each data record. For example, the Title band contains today's date.

3. Observe that the Detail band has stretched to accommodate all the selected records.

4. Look at the Group Header. The industry type of the first group is "AUTO."

5. Observe the calculated volume in the Group Footer. You may want to do a quick check to see if the result is correct.

6. Select **More** to see more and select **Done** when you are done with the preview.

REPORT WRITER OBJECTS

When you add a data field to a report layout, or create a graphic on it, or type a string of text, each of these entries becomes a Report Writer object. So a report layout is actually composed of objects. In the STOCK.FRX illustration, the *pe* field, the box around the report title, and the text "Total Value Today:" are objects.

Before you can modify an existing object, you have to select the object first. Then you can change the size of the object or move or delete the object.

SELECTING AN OBJECT   Try to select the object "Total Volume Today:"

1. Click on any character of this text string or move the cursor to this string and then press **Spacebar**. The object becomes highlighted.

DESELECTING AN OBJECT   If you do not want to modify the object after selection, or you are done with the modification, you can deselect it.

1. Click on any empty spot on the Report Layout window or press **Spacebar**. The highlight disappears.

SELECTING MULTIPLE OBJECTS   You can select multiple objects in one operation. This process is particularly useful if you want to modify them the same way. Try to select the field headings in the Page Header band.

1. Press and hold down **Shift**, click on each of the objects or move the cursor to each object and press **Spacebar**. Then release **Shift**. Notice that each of the target objects is now highlighted.

   You can deselect multiple objects by clicking on an empty spot on the Report Layout window or by pressing **Spacebar**.

MOVING AN OBJECT   Try to move *date( )*.

1. With the mouse:
   a. Drag *date( )* with the mouse until the object is at the desired position, then release the button.
   b. Click on an empty spot to deselect the object.

2. With the keyboard:
   a. Select the object.
   b. Press **Left, Right, Up,** or **Down Arrow** to move the object to the desired position.
   c. Deselect the object.

DELETING AN OBJECT   Try to delete the box of the report title.

1. Select the box, then press **Backspace** or **Del**.

EDITING A TEXT OBJECT   Try to change "Total Volume Today:" to "Total Traded This Group:"

1. Click on the "V" of "Volume" or move the cursor to this position. Type **Traded This Group:**. Press **Del** to delete "Volume Today:." Press **Enter**.
2. Press **Esc** to close STOCK.FRX. Click on **Yes** to discard the changes, so your original file remains intact.

CREATING A REPORT LAYOUT

This exercise is to create a report layout for reporting on the data of SEMINAR.DBF. Include the following fields in the report layout: *city, jobtype, lastname, gender, howmany,* and *lastdate.* You can use the following figure as a guide in positioning the objects.

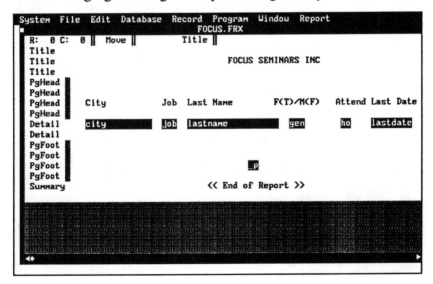

Here are the steps to follow.

1. Select the File menu and **Open** option.
2. Select the **Database** popup.
3. Select SEMINAR.DBF and then **Open**.

TIP: If SEMINAR.DBF is dimmed, it is already opened. Press Esc instead of Open and then do step 4.

4. a. Press **Ctrl+F2** to open the Command window.

   b. Type **SELECT SEMINAR** and press **Enter**. This command activates the database.

   c. Select the Window menu and **Hide** option to hide the Command window.

5. Select the File menu and **New** option.
6. Select **Report** and then **OK**. The Report Layout window in the default format appears.
7. Add the Title and Summary bands.

   a. Select the Report menu and **Title/Summary** option.

   b. Select **Title Band** and **Summary Band** from the dialog as shown in the following figure. Select **OK**.

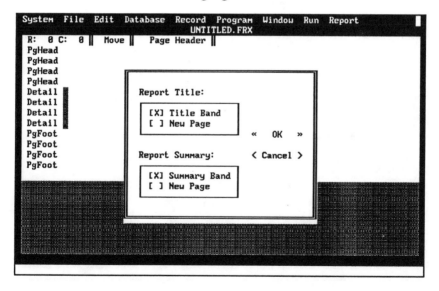

8. Add more lines to the Title band.

   a. With the mouse:

   (1) Drag the title of the Title band downward until there is sufficient space in this band for the title.

   b. With the keyboard:

   (1) Press **Tab** to move the cursor to the Title band.

   (2) Select the Report menu and **Add Line** option. FoxPro adds a line to this band.

   (3) Repeat step 8.b(2) to add more lines as necessary.

9. Add the title:

   a. Click on the position in the Title band for the first letter of the title or move the cursor to this position.

   b. Type **FOCUS SEMINARS INC** and press **Enter**. Notice that the title of this band becomes brightened.

10. Add the field *city*.

    a. Click on the position of the *city* field on the Report Layout window or move the cursor to this position.

    b. Select the Report menu and **Field** option. A dialog appears. See the following figure.

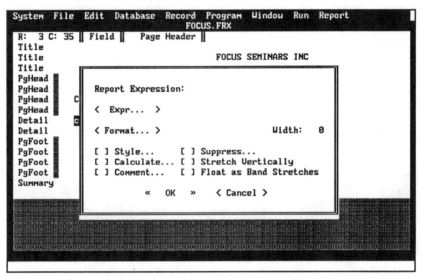

c. Click on the text area next to Expr. . . or move the cursor to this position. Type **seminar.city** and press **Enter**.

d. Click on the text area next to Format. . . or move the cursor to this position. Type **XXXXXXXXXXXXX** (that is, 13 X's) to represent the desired width of this field on the report.

e. Notice that this width specifies the width you want *seminar.city* to appear in the report layout. It does not affect the width of this field in SEMINAR.DBF.

f. Select **OK**.

11. Repeat step 10 to add fields **seminar.jobtype, seminar.lastname, seminar.gender, seminar.howmany,** and **seminar.lastdate** to the Detail band. Type 18 **X**'s for the width of *seminar.lastname*. For the other four fields, the widths selected by the Report Writer from SEMINAR.DBF are acceptable.

12. Notice that the names of some of these fields are truncated in the report layout because of the widths selected. The truncation does not affect your results.

13. Click on the Page Header band where you want the field heading "City" to be, or move the cursor to this position. Type **City** and press **Enter**.

14. Repeat step 13 for the other five field headings.

15. Click on the Summary band where you want the text to be or move the cursor to this position. Type **<< End of Report >>**. Press **Enter**.

16. Click on the Page Footer band where you want the page number to be, or move the cursor to this position. Type **_pageno**. Press **Enter**. Notice the underscore. *_pageno* is a variable provided by FoxPro for numbering pages automatically.

17. Select the Report menu and **Page Preview** option. Your screen should look like the following figure.

NOTE

To eliminate extra space between lines, click on the bottom of the Detail band and drag upward to eliminate the desired number of extra lines (opposite of what you did to add lines to the Title band).

```
 System  File  Edit  Database  Record  Program  Window  Run  Report
 ■                                Preview
 ═══════════════════════════════════════════════════════════════════

                          FOCUS SEMINARS INC


   City          Job  Last Name        F(T)/M(F)  Attend  Last Date

   Jersey City   MGM  Motti              .F.        1      06/14/88

   Newark        ECO  Lewis              .T.        4      02/18/91

   Jersey City   ECO  Andrews            .T.        3      02/18/91

   Jersey City   MGM  Lobo               .T.        2      09/21/90

   Newark        ACC  Davidson           .F.        2      09/21/90

   Newark        ECO  Bohm               .T.        2      09/21/90

   Jersey City   ECO  Slater             .T.        2      02/18/91
 « Done »  < More >   Column:    0
 ◄►                                                                 ►
```

18. Select **More** to see more. Select **Done** to exit the Page Preview window.

19. Select the File menu and **Save As** option. Type **SECT8_1** and press **Ctrl+Enter** to save the file.

You have successfully created a report layout. Is reporting on your data easy? You can enhance this report in Section 9.

Section 9

ENHANCING A REPORT

INTRODUCING MORE FEATURES
OF THE REPORT WRITER

This section introduces you to additional features for enhancing the quality of a report. These features include:

- Page layout
- Format
- Template
- Font styles
- Graphics
- Comment

The use of these features is optional. You can print a report without using any of these options.

PAGE LAYOUT   It deals with the paper size, margins, paper feed, and so forth.

FORMAT   You can select the format in which the value of a data field is presented in the output. There is one set of selections for character fields and one for numeric fields. The following two tables show the more frequently used format selections.

Format Options for Character Fields

Option	Effect on Output
Alpha Only	Only alphabetic characters allowed
To Upper Case	All characters expressed in uppercase
Trim	Remove all leading and trailing spaces in the value of a data field
Right Align	Print data flush right in the field (The default is flush left.)
Center	Print data in the middle of the field

Format Options for Numeric Fields

Option	Effect on Output
Left Justify	Print data flush left in the field (The default is flush right.)
Blank if Zero	Do not print if field value is zero
(Negative)	Print a negative value within parentheses
CR if Positive	Print CR (for credit) after the number if value is positive
DB if Negative	Print DB (for debit) after the number if value is negative
Leading Zeros	Print all leading zeros
Currency	Display currency symbols for selection
Scientific	Display scientific notations for selection

TEMPLATE This feature can be considered as part of the format feature. You use it to specify the width of an output field, display the decimal point, and the like. The following table shows common template options and their effects on the input and output.

Template Options

Code	Effect on Input and Output
A	Accept and display alphabetic characters only
N	Accept and display letters and digits only
X	Accept and display any character type
9	Accept and display digits and signs for numeric fields
#	Display digits, signs, and blanks
$	Display the dollar sign at a fixed position
$$	Display the dollar sign in a floating position
.	Specify the position of the decimal point in a numeric field
,	Specify digits left of the decimal point of a numeric field

Examples The following table illustrates the use of the templates.

Illustration of Use of Templates

Data	Template Used	Output
Room 215	AAAAAAAA	Not valid (215 are not alphabetic letters)
Room 215	NNNNNNNN	Room 215
Room 215	NNNNNN	Room 2
Room #215	XXXXXXXXXXX	Room #215
4983	99999	4983
4983	999	*** (Not enough space)
4983	9,999	4,983
4983	9999.9	498.3

FONT STYLES You can use a variety of font styles for data fields. The styles include bold, italic, underline, superscript, subscript, and left or center or right alignment of the data.

GRAPHICS   You can draw boxes and horizontal and vertical lines among the text of a report.

COMMENT   Each object of a report layout may have a comment. This is text that serves as a reminder for the report designer about the object. A comment is not printed with a report.

USING ENHANCEMENT FEATURES

You may want to do the following exercises to enhance the report layout prepared in Section 8.

DESIGNING PAGE LAYOUT   You want to print the full report on letter size paper. The top and bottom margins are 10 blank lines each; the left margin seven columns, and the right margin five columns. You do not want to eject a page before or after printing. The page header is required on every page, so the Plain Page option is not used.

Here are the steps to follow.

1. Select the Report menu and **Page Layout** option. A dialog appears. See the following figure.

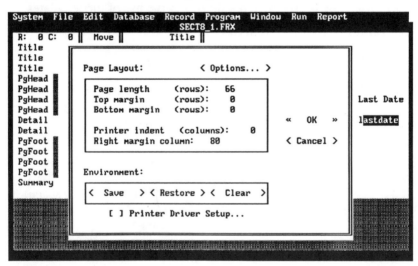

2. Move the cursor to the text area of Top margin. Type **10** and press **Enter**.

3. Repeat step 2 for the Bottom margin.

4. Type **7** in the text area for Printer indent and press **Enter**.

5. Type **68** in the text area for the Right margin column and press **Enter**.

6. Select **Options...** to look at the available options.

7. Press **Esc** when done. There is no need to modify the options.

8. Select **OK** to return to the Report Design window.

SPECIFYING FORMATS AND TEMPLATES You want the names of cities in uppercase and to leave a blank space if a client has not attended any seminar in the report period.

Here are the steps to follow.

1. Open the dialog of the field object of *seminar.city*: Double-click on the object or move the cursor to this object and then press **Enter**. The Report Expression dialog appears to allow editing of the field.

TIP: Step 1 is the general step for bringing forward a field object of an existing report layout for editing.

2. Check the data field name appearing in the dialog to ensure that you are editing the right data field.

3. Select **Format....** A dialog appears. See the following figure.

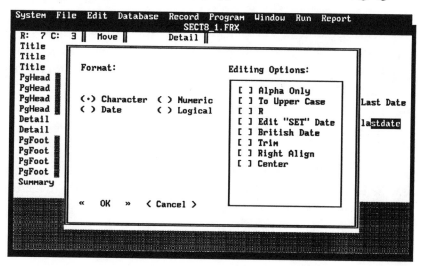

77

4. Notice that Character has been preselected by the Report Writer.

5. Select **To Upper Case** and **Trim** in the Editing Options area.

6. Leave the Format text area as it is. It echoes the format XXXXXXXXXXXXX you chose when creating this field.

7. Select **OK** to return to the Report Expression dialog.

8. Select **Style. . . .** A dialog appears. See the following figure.

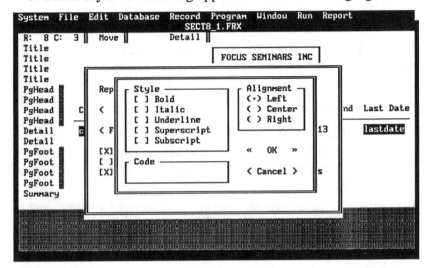

9. Select **Bold** and then select **OK** to return to the Report Expression dialog.

10. Select **Comment**. The Comment text editing window appears.

11. Click on the text area or move the cursor to this position. Type **Field width in data table is 24. City names stored in uppercase format.** Select **OK**.

12. Click **OK** twice to return to the Report Layout window.

13. Bring forward the dialog of field object *seminar.howmany* for editing.

14. Select **Format. . . .** The Format dialog appears.

15. Select **Numeric**. Notice that the Editing Options of a numeric field are different from those of a character field.

16. Select **Blank if Zero** and **OK**.

17. Type **99** in the text area next to Format. . . and press **Enter**.

18. Select **OK** to return to the Report Layout window.

19. Click on the position where you want "Date:" to be in the Title band or move the cursor to this position. Type **Date:** and press **Enter**.

20. Click on the position for the *date( )* field or move the cursor to this position. Select the Report menu and **Field** option. Type **date( )** in the Expr text area in the dialog and press **Enter**. Type **8** in the Width text area. Select **OK** to return to the Report Layout window.

ADDING GRAPHICS   You want to draw a box around the seminar firm's name, date, and a line underneath the data headings. Here are the steps to follow.

1. Click above and to the left of the title text to position the upper left corner of the desired box, or move the cursor to this position.

2. Select the Report menu and **Box** option. A small blinking box appears.

3. Drag the mouse down and to the right below the *date( )* to define the box, and then release the button. Or press the **Right** and **Down Arrows** to stretch the box and then press **Enter**.

4. Adjust the box size.

   a. With the mouse:

      (1) Press **Ctrl** and click on the box and drag the mouse to change the size of the box. Release the button when the box has the desired size.

   b. With the keyboard:

      (1) Move the cursor to the box.

      (2) Press **Ctrl+Spacebar**. The box blinks. Press **Right, Down, Up,** or **Left Arrow** to adjust the size of the box. Then press **Enter**. The box stops blinking.

5. Adjust the box position: Click and drag the box to the desired position. Or move the cursor to the position, press **Spacebar**, and press **Left, Right, Up,** or **Down Arrow** to move the box. Press **Spacebar**.

6. Underline the data headings in the Page Header band.

   a. Click on the position for the left end of the underline or move the cursor to this position.

   b. Select the Report menu and **Box** option.

   c. Press **Up Arrow** to shrink the blinking box to a line.

      d. Press **Right Arrow** to stretch the line. Press **Enter** when the line has the desired length.

7. Center the report title:

    a. Select the report title box.

    b. Select the Report menu and **Center** option to position the box. Deselect the box.

    c. Multiselect the other objects to be enclosed by the box. Move them inside the box. Deselect the objects.

SAVING FILE AND PRINTING Follow these steps to save the file and print. If you do not wish to print, skip steps 3 through 6.

1. Select the File menu and **Save As** option.

2. Type **SECT09_1** and press **Ctrl+Enter** to save the file.

3. Select the Database menu and **Report** option. A dialog appears. See the following figure.

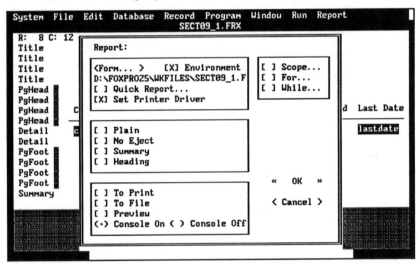

4. Select **To Print**.

5. Select **Console Off** if you do not want the report to be displayed on the screen during printing. This speeds up the printing process.

6. Select **OK** to start printing.

7. Press **Esc** to close SECT09_1.FRX.

How do you like your report design and the Report Writer features?

Section 10

REPORTING RQBE RESULTS

INTRODUCTION

RQBE and the Report Writer are powerful enough when they work alone. They are even more powerful when you use them together. This section teaches you how to take advantage of their joint capabilities. The idea is to ask RQBE to do your query and the Report Writer to produce the query report using a report layout of your choice. You create your report layout through RQBE and save it. Subsequently, you can modify the layout as you did in Sections 8 and 9, independently of RQBE, if you do not add new data fields to the report layout.

You can try the following exercises. The database to be used is SEMINAR.DBF.

PRESELECTED AND SORTED LIST OF ADDRESSES

In this exercise, you prepare a list of addresses of those clients who attended seminars in 1991 and 1992 and do not live in Atlantic City (too far from the seminar firm). Arrange the addresses according to the clients' zip codes to facilitate presorting required in bulk mailing. Also print the zip codes in bold style. You do three tasks to accomplish your goal. The first task is to create a report layout through RQBE. The second task is to modify the report layout. The third task is to do the query and print the address list.

CREATING A REPORT LAYOUT THROUGH RQBE

1. Select the File menu and **Open** option.

2. Select **SEMINAR.DBF** and **Open**.

TIP: If SEMINAR.DBF is dimmed, it is already opened. Press Esc instead of Open and then do step 3.

3. a. Press **Ctrl+F2** to open the Command window.

   b. Type **SELECT SEMINAR** and press **Enter**. This command activates the database.

   c. Select the Window menu and **Hide** option to hide the Command window.

4. Select the File menu and **New** option.

5. Select **Query** and **OK**. The RQBE window appears.

6. Choose **Select Fields** and then in the RQBE field selection dialog select **Remove All**.

7. Move *morename, lastname, title, employer, street, city, state,* and *zip* to the Selected Output list. Select **OK**.

8. Select **Report/Label** from the Output To popup. Select **Options. . . .** A dialog appears. See the following figure.

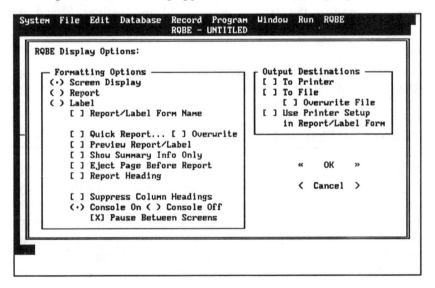

9. Select **Report** and **Quick Report**. A dialog appears. See the
   following figure.

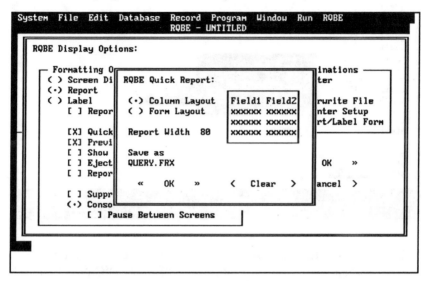

10. Select **Form Layout**. Notice that the layout in the small box
    changes with your selection.

11. Type **SECT10_1.FRX** in the text area next to Save As. (Delete
    the unwanted word "QUERY.") Press **Ctrl+Enter** to return to
    the previous dialog.

12. Notice that FoxPro has added SECT10_1.FRX to this dialog.

13. Select **OK** to return to the RQBE window.

14. Select **Do Query**. FoxPro automatically lets you preview the
    output. Select **More** to see more and **Done** to return to the RQBE
    window.

TIP: You must do the query in order to create the quick report. FoxPro
saves the file automatically.

15. Select the File menu and save the query file as **SECT10_1**.

16. Press **Esc** to close the RQBE window.

MODIFYING THE REPORT LAYOUT

1. Select the File menu and **Open** option.

2. Select **Report** in the Type popup. Select **SECT10_1.FRX** and
   Open. The report layout appears. See the following figure.

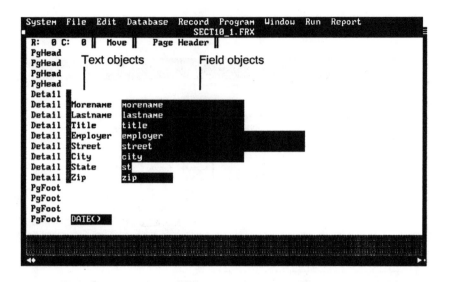

3. Multiselect the text objects (not the field objects) "Morename," "Lastname," "Title," "Employer," "Street," "City," "State," and "Zip" in the Detail band. Press **Backspace** to delete them.

4. Combine the data fields *morename* and *lastname*.

   a. Double-click on *morename* or move the cursor to this position and then press **Enter**. The Report Expression dialog appears.

   b. Type **TRIM(morename)+" "+lastname** in the text area next to Expr. . . and press **Enter**.

   c. Move the cursor to the text area next to Format. . . . Type 48 **X**'s to represent the combined width of *morename* and *lastname*. Press **Enter**.

   ### NOTE
   The text area may appear to be too short for the 48 X's. What actually happens is that, as you type, this text area scrolls to make room for all the X's, only the scrolling is not apparent to the eye.

   d. Select **OK**.

5. Select the *lastname* field and press **Backspace** to delete it. Move the remaining fields upward to take up the blank line.

TIP: Multiselect these fields and drag them upward or press the **Up Arrow**. Then deselect the objects.

6. Follow step 4 to change *city* to **TRIM(city)+" "+state**. Type 26 **X**'s for the format.

7. Delete *state* in the line below and move *zip* to take up the blank line.

8. Bring forward the Report Expression dialog of *zip*. Select **Style**. A dialog appears.

9. Select **Bold** and then **OK**.

10. Select **OK** to return to the Report Layout window.

11. Select *date( )* in the Page Footer band and delete it. Your finished layout should look like the following figure.

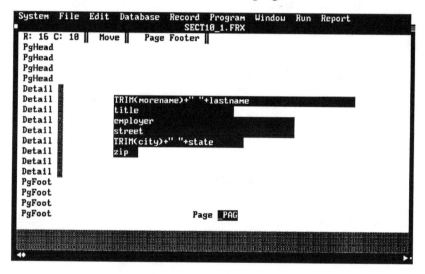

12. Select the File menu and **Save** option to save the changes.

13. Press **Esc** to close the Report Layout window.

DOING QUERY AND PRINTING THE ADDRESS LIST

1. Select the File menu and **Open** option.

2. Select **Query** from the Type popup and select **SECT10_1.QPR** and **Open**.

3. Select **Order By**. The RQBE Order By dialog appears. Move *zip* to the Ordering Criteria list. Select **OK**.

4. Select *seminar.city* from the Field Name popup of the Selection Criteria box. Select the NOT comparator. Type **Atlantic City** in the Example text area.

5. Move the cursor to the second line of the Selection Criteria box.

6. Select *lastdate* from the Field Name popup. Select the More Than comparator. Type **12/31/90** in the Example text area.

7. Select **Do Query**. The Page Preview window appears. Your screen should look like the following figure.

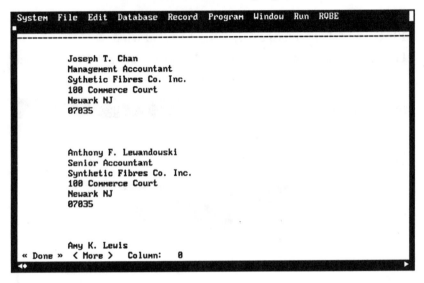

8. Select **More** to see more and **Done** to close the Page Preview window. Skip steps 9 through 11 if you do not want to print the address list.

9. Select **Options...** to open the RQBE Display Options dialog.

10. Deselect **Preview Report/Label** and select **To Printer** in the Output Destinations area. Select **OK**.

11. Select **Do Query**. RQBE sends the output to the printer using the report layout.

12. Select the File menu and **Save** option to save the changes.

13. Press **Esc** to close the RQBE window.

You have successfully created an address list that is preselected and sorted. You have an efficient way of handling business mailing.

DATA GROUPING

In Section 6, you asked RQBE to calculate some group statistics for you. Now you can be more ambitious. You can include details of individual clients in the group statistics so you can get an idea of who is in the statistics. For the sake of comparison with Section 6, you group the data in the same way as before. That is: group by *city* and within each city, by *jobtype*. The statistics are: count, sum, average, and maximum. For details of an individual client, include the following data fields: *lastname*, *howmany*, *gender*, and *lastdate*.

You can start the exercise with the query file GROUPING.QPR and the report file GROUPING.FRX in the diskette supplied with this book to save some time. The report file was created in a similar manner as in the previous exercise.

The complete exercise consists of two tasks: creating group header and group footer bands in the report layout, and doing a query with the modified report layout.

CREATING GROUP HEADER AND GROUP FOOTER BANDS

1. Select the File menu and **Open** option.
2. Select **Report** from the Type popup.
3. Select **GROUPING.FRX** and **Open**. The Report Layout window appears. See the following figure.

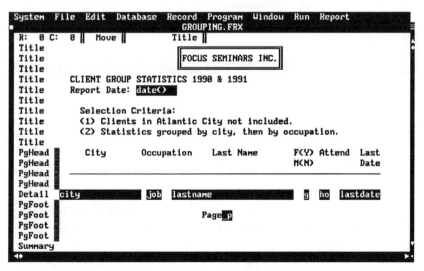

4. Select the Report menu and **Data Grouping** option.

5. Select **Add**. A dialog appears.

6. Type **city** in the text area next to Group and select **OK**.

7. Repeat steps 5 and 6 for **jobtype**.

8. Select **OK** to return to the Report Layout window.

9. Notice that the 2-jobtype Group band is nested within the 1-city Group band.

10. Add lines to the Group Footer band.

   a. With the mouse:

      (1) Click on the title of the 2-jobtype Group Footer band and drag the mouse to create sufficient space in this band. Use the following figure as a guide.

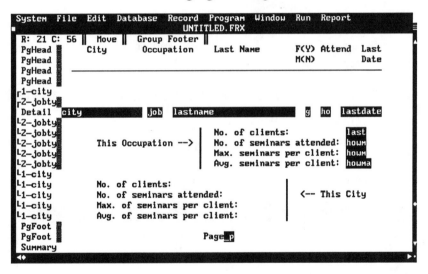

      (2) Repeat step 10a(1) for the 1-city Group Footer band.

   b. With the keyboard:

      (1) Move the cursor to the 2-jobtype Group Footer band.

      (2) Select the Report menu and **Add Line** option to add one line to this band.

      (3) Repeat step 10b(2) to add as many lines as necessary.

      (4) Repeat steps 10b(1) to (3) to add lines to the 1-city Group Footer band.

11. Type all the text in the 2-jobtype and 1-city Group Footer bands.

12. Click on the position for the field *lastname* in the 2-jobtype Group Footer band.

13. Select the Report menu and **Field** option. A dialog appears.

14. Type **lastname** in the text area next to Expr. . . .

15. Select **Calculate**. A dialog appears.

16. Select **Count**. Accept *jobtype* in the Reset popup. Select **OK**.

17. Select **Format. . . .** A dialog appears.

18. Select **Numeric**. Type **9999** in the text area below Format. Select **Blank if Zero**.

19. Select **OK** in each of the two dialogs to return to the Report Layout window.

20. Repeat steps 12 through 19 for the following three fields, but type **howmany** instead of *lastname*.

No.	Format **9999**
Max.	Format **9999**
Avg.	Format **999.9**

21. Repeat steps 12 through 20 for the same four fields in the 1-city Group Footer band. Select *city* from the Reset popup.

22. Select the File menu and save the file as SECT10_2.FRX.

23. Press **Esc** to close the Report Layout window.

QUERYING FOR DATA GROUPING REPORT

1. Select the File menu and **Open** option, then select **Query** from the Type popup.

2. Select **GROUPING.QPR** and **Open** to bring forward the query file.

3. Select **Options. . .** to bring forward the report RQBE Display Options dialog.

4. Change GROUPING.FRX to **SECT10_2.FRX**.

5. Select **OK** to return to the RQBE window.

6. Select **Do Query**.

7. Select **Done** to close the Preview window.

8. Select the File menu and save the query file as SECT10_2.QPR.

9. Print the report if you want, as you did in the previous exercise.

10. Press **Esc** to close the RQBE window.

At this point, you have learned the techniques most often used in database management by end-users. But you can increase your capability of using FoxPro in the sections which follow. You may want to move on.

Section 11

MULTIPLE DATABASES AND VARIABLES

ABOUT RELATIONAL DATABASES

Let us suppose that the seminar firm wants additional information on the seminars and the clients for marketing purposes. The firm wants reports on the types and chronology of seminars attended by each client, and statistics of attendance, revenue, and profit.

To be able to produce these reports, the following data fields are required (the names in parentheses are the data field names):

- Seminar I.D. number (*semnum*)
- Seminar title (*semname*)
- Seminar date (*semdate*)
- Venue (*venue*)
- Registration fee per person (*fee*)
- Cost of seminar (*cost*)

You could modify SEMINAR.DBF to include these data fields, but this approach is not efficient. Visualize the data entry task. Suppose a seminar is attended by 100 people. Do we want to enter the seminar title, date, venue, registration fee, and cost into the record of every client? You say "No," because there are several problems of doing so:

- Wasteful efforts of data entry
- Potential discrepancy in repeated data due to human error

- Wasteful use of data storage space

An alternative approach is to create two additional databases and use them along with SEMINAR.DBF. See their structures in the following table. These two databases, named ATTENDEE.DBF and COURSE.DBF, are on the diskette supplied with this book. You can browse them if you want.

In this alternative approach, you need to enter the details of a new seminar once only in COURSE.DBF regardless of the number of attendees. Similarly, you need to enter details of a new client once only in SEMINAR.DBF. For a continuing client who registers for a seminar, all you need to enter are just the two data fields *id_num* and *semnum* in ATTENDEE.DBF. Is this approach simple?

Database Structure of ATTENDEE.DBF

Field Name	Type	Width	Index
id_num	C	4	Y
semnum	C	6	Y

Database Structure of COURSE.DBF

Field Name	Type	Width	Index
semnum	C	6	Y
semname	C	24	
semdate	D	8	
venue	C	24	
fee	N	4	
cost	N	7	

How do these three databases work together? First, you relate one database with another, using a data field that is common to both databases. See the relations in the following figure. COURSE.DBF is related to ATTENDEE.DBF by the field *semnum*. SEMINAR.DBF is related to ATTENDEE.DBF by the field *id_num*. Databases related in this manner are called relational databases. COURSE.DBF is related to SEMINAR.DBF indirectly by the database ATTENDEE.DBF.

Notice that although the relations exist among the three databases, the databases are not joined physically as limbs are to the torso. Rather, they are joined by computer logic; that is, the field common to both databases. You can establish the relations with the help of RQBE. You can add records to a relational database or edit existing records as if the relation does not exist.

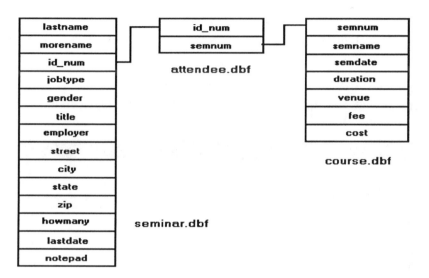

Let us see how RQBE retrieves information after the relations are established. Suppose you want a list of last names of clients who attended the seminar named "MGM201." RQBE searches ATTENDEE.DBF first to pick up all records which contain "MGM201" in the data field *attendee.semnum*. RQBE next searches all records in SEMINAR.DBF and picks those whose *seminar.id_num* match *attendee.id_num* of the records picked in the first search. Finally, RQBE presents the last names of the records picked in the second search, and this is the list you want.

The searches just described may seem to be cumbersome to you, but RQBE is good at doing this. In fact, relational databases are widely used in real world applications. You can now put RQBE to work for you, using relational databases.

USING RQBE WITH RELATIONAL DATABASES

In this exercise, you want to prepare a list of all seminars and the clients attending each of them. Include the following fields in the output: *lastname, semnum, semname,* and *semdate.* Here are the steps to follow.

1. Select the File menu and **Open** option.
2. Select the **Database** type and select **COURSE.DBF**, then **Open**.
3. Select the File menu and **New** option.
4. Select **Query** and **OK**. A new RQBE window appears.
5. Select **Add**. Select **ATTENDEE.DBF** from the Open dialog and select **Open**. A dialog appears. See the following figure.

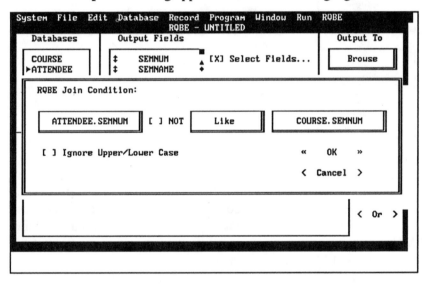

6. Select *attendee.semnum* from the leftmost popup if necessary.
7. Select **Exactly Like** from the comparator popup in the middle of the dialog.
8. Select *course.semnum* from the rightmost popup if necessary.
9. Select **OK**.
10. Repeat steps 5 through 9, but select SEMINAR.DBF as the database to be added, *seminar.id_num* from the leftmost popup, and *attendee.id_num* from the rightmost popup.

TIP: You cannot select *seminar.dbf* to join with *course.dbf* because there is no data field that is common to both of them.

11. Notice that the relations are echoed in the Selection Criteria box, and an arrow bar appears to the left of the data field that establishes a relation.

12. Choose **Select Fields**.

13. Remove all fields from the Selected Output list. Move *seminar.lastname*, *course.semnum*, *course.semname*, and *course.semdate* to the Selected Output list. Select **OK**.

14. Select **Order By**.

15. Move *course.semnum* and *seminar.lastname* to the Ordering Criteria list. Select **OK**.

16. Select **Do Query**. Your results should look like the following figure.

```
System  File  Edit  Database  Record  Program  Window  Run  Browse
                              QUERY
 Lastname              Semnum Semname                   Semdate

 Condi                 MGM101 Team Building              06/15/90
 Kelly                 MGM101 Team Building              06/15/90
 Lewis                 MGM101 Team Building              06/15/90
 Slater                MGM101 Team Building              06/15/90
 Andrews               MGM201 Business Ethics            02/18/91
 Chan                  MGM201 Business Ethics            02/18/91
 Condi                 MGM201 Business Ethics            02/18/91
 Kelly                 MGM201 Business Ethics            02/18/91
 Lewandowski           MGM201 Business Ethics            02/18/91
 Lewis                 MGM201 Business Ethics            02/18/91
 Marks                 MGM201 Business Ethics            02/18/91
 Slater                MGM201 Business Ethics            02/18/91
 Motti                 PER005 Retirement Planning        06/14/88
 Andrews               PER101 Communication Skills       05/14/90
 Bohm                  PER101 Communication Skills       05/14/90
 Davidson              PER101 Communication Skills       05/14/90
 Lewis                 PER101 Communication Skills       05/14/90
 Lobo                  PER101 Communication Skills       05/14/90
 Chan                  PER102 Communication Skills       11/25/90
 Davis                 PER102 Communication Skills       11/25/90
```

17. Press **Esc** to return to the RQBE window.

18. Select the File menu and save the file as SECT11_1.

SUPPRESSING REPEATED VALUES   The query results you just saw repeated the details of the same seminar for every attendee. You can eliminate the repetition with the Report Writer. Here are the steps to follow.

1. Select **Report/Label** from the Output To popup.
2. Select **Options** to bring forward the report dialog.
3. Select **Report** and **Quick Report**.
4. Type **SECT11_1.FRX** in the Save As text area and select **OK**.
5. Select **OK** to return to the RQBE window.
6. Select **Do Query** to create the quick report.
7. Select **Done** after viewing the page.
8. Select the File menu and **Save** option to save the changes in the query file.
9. Press **Esc** to close the RQBE window.
10. Select the File menu and **Open** option.
11. Select **Report** from the Type popup, then select **SECT11_1.FRX** and **Open**.
12. Double-click on the *semnum* field or move the cursor to this object and press **Enter** to open its dialog.
13. Select **Suppress**. A dialog appears.
14. Accept **End of Report** in the Reset popup. Select **On** in the Suppress Repeated Values box.
15. Select **OK** twice to return to the Report Layout window.
16. Repeat steps 12 through 15 for *semname* and *semdate*.
17. Select the Report menu and **Page Preview** option. Your screen should look like the following figure. There is no more repetition.

```
 System  File  Edit  Database  Record  Program  Window  Run  Report
                               Preview
--------------------------------------------------------------------------
Lastname                  Semnum Semname                Semdate


Condi                     MGM101 Team Building          06/15/90
Kelly
Lewis
Slater
Andrews                   MGM201 Business Ethics        02/18/91
Chan
Condi
Kelly
Lewandouski
Lewis
Marks
Slater
Motti                     PER005 Retirement Planning    06/14/88
Andrews                   PER101 Communication Skills   05/14/90
Bohm
Davidson
 « Done »  < More >   Column:    0
```

Notice that you can also use RQBE to preview and print the report.

18. Select **Done** to return to the Report Layout window when done.

19. Select the File menu and **Save** option to save the report layout file.

20. Press **Esc** to close the Report Layout window.

VARIABLES

A *variable* is another kind of "field" used for storing a value so the value can be made available for computer processing when needed. Like a data field, a variable must have a name for identification. The naming of a variable follows the same convention as for a data field. A variable is not part of a database structure, however. You can create variables whenever you need them.

An example of use of variables is a mathematical formula. For example, you can write a formula for the area of a rectangle as follows:

*area = length * height*

where *area*, *length*, and *height* are variables and the asterisk (*) is the multiplication sign. In one computation, you can store 10 in *length* and 5 in *height*. Then *area* becomes 50. In another computation, you can store 120 in *length* and 40 in *height* and *area* becomes 4800.

A variable can also store a character string such as "Pacific Ocean" or a logical value, that is, T or F. In the next exercise, you use variables in a report.

USING VARIABLES

In this exercise, you want to produce a report for the seminar firm. The report contains the following information.

Information on each individual seminar:

- The I.D. number, title, date, unit registration fee
- The attendance figure, broken down by clients' occupations
- The total revenue, cost, and profit

Information on all seminars:

- The total number of seminars done
- The total attendance figure
- The total revenue, cost, profit
- The average profit per seminar and per attendee

VARIABLE NAMES The following table shows the variables you need:

Variable Name	Meaning and Use
sem_fee	Total revenue from each seminar
one_sem	Count of each seminar
all_sem	Count of total number of seminars
all_id	Count of total number of attendees in all seminars
all_fee	Total revenue from all seminars
all_cost	Total cost of all seminars

CREATING VARIABLES You can use the query file named RELATE2.QPR and the report layout file named RELATE2.FRX from the diskette supplied with this book to complete your work. RELATE2.FRX was modified from a quick report created through RELATE2.QPR. Their windows look like the following figures.

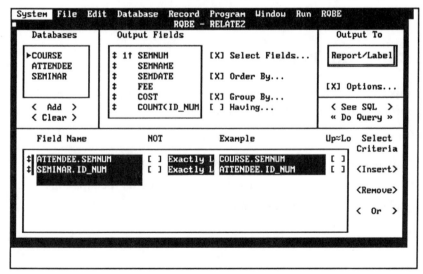

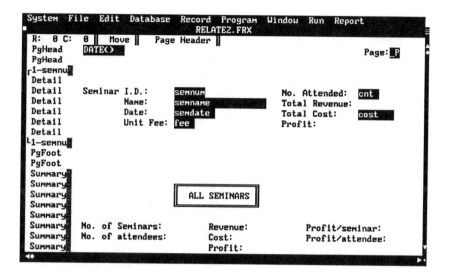

1. Select the File menu and **Open** option.
2. Select **RELATE2.FRX** and **Open**.
3. Select the Report menu and **Variables** option.
4. Select **Add**. A dialog appears. See the following figure.

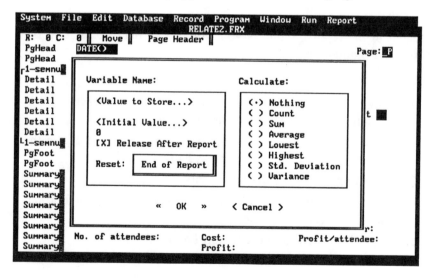

5. Type **sem_fee** in the text area next to Variable Name and press **Enter**.

6. Type **fee*cnt** in the text area below Value to Store and press **Enter**. *Cnt* is the number of attendees counted by RQBE. The asterisk (*) is the multiplication sign.

7. Select *course.semnum* from the Reset popup.

8. Select **OK** to return to the first dialog.

9. Repeat steps 4 through 8 for the following variables.

Variable Name	Value to Store	Calculate	Reset
one_sem	cnt/cnt	Nothing	*course.semnum*
all_sem	one_sem	Sum	End of Report
all_id	cnt	Sum	End of Report
all_fee	sem_fee	Sum	End of Report
all_cost	cost	Sum	End of Report

10. Select **OK** to return to the Report Layout window.

PLACING VARIABLES You can place the variables you just created in the report layout as you would with data fields. Use the following figure as a guide.

Here are the steps to follow.

1. Click on the position for the field next to "Total Revenue:" in the Detail band or move the cursor to this position.

2. Select the Report menu and **Field** option. Type **sem_fee** in the text area next to Expr. . . and press **Enter**.

3. Select **Format. . . .** A dialog appears.

4. Select **Numeric**. Type **99999** in the text area below Format. Select **Blank if Zero**. Select **OK**.

5. Select **OK** to return to the Report Layout window.

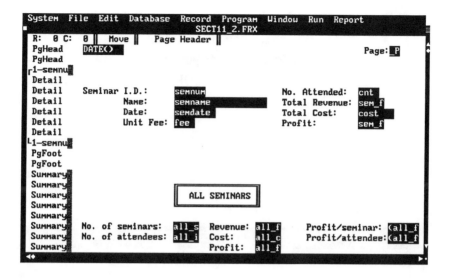

6. Repeat steps 1 through 5 to place **sem_fee-cost** next to "Profit:" in this band.

7. Repeat steps 1 through 5 to place the following fields in the Summary band.

Place Field Next to	Type Text Next to Expr. . .	Format
"No. of Seminars"	**all_sem**	**99999**
"No. of Attendees"	**all_id**	**99999**
"Revenue"	**all_fee**	**99999**
"Cost"	**all_cost**	**99999**
"Profit"	**all_fee-all_cost**	**99999**
"Profit/seminar"	**(all_fee-all_cost)/all_sem**	**9999.9**
"Profit/attendee"	**(all_fee-all_cost)/all_id**	**9999.9**

8. Select the File menu and save the report layout file as SECT11_2.

9. Do query with RELATE2.QPR.

    a. Select the File menu and **Open** option.

    b. Select **Query** from the Type popup.

    c. Double-click on RELATE2.QPR to open the file. The RQBE-RELATE2 window opens.

    d. Click on **Options** to open its dialog. Change the report file name to SECT11_2.FRX. Select **OK** to return to the RQBE-RELATE2 window.

    e. Select **Do Query**. The Page Preview window appears. Your screen should look like the following figure. Do a manual check of the arithmetic if you want.

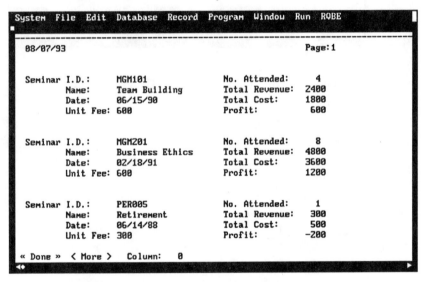

    f. Select **Done** to close the Page Preview window and return to the RQBE-RELATE2 window.

10. Save the query file as SECT11_2.QPR if you want and leave RELATE2.QPR intact.

11. Press **Esc** to close the RQBE window.

12. Press **Esc** to close the report window.

In this exercise, you used RQBE to set up the relations of multiple databases and do queries. You could include selection criteria in your queries as you did with a single database. Congratulations! You have accomplished very complex tasks. You have seen how fantastic RQBE is. You may want to move on to try another powerful tool, the Screen Builder.

Section 12

BUILDING A DIALOG SCREEN

ABOUT THE SCREEN BUILDER

You can use FoxPro's Screen Builder to build a screen which allows communications to take place between the user and the screen at runtime. When the screen is running, it displays output information and accepts input data from the user. A user-built dialog screen can be as sophisticated as a dialog of FoxPro.

Like a report layout, a screen layout is composed of objects which can be strings of text, data fields, variables, or graphics. These Screen Builder objects behave exactly as the Report Writer objects. In addition, the Screen Builder provides five other types of objects. These are:

- Radio button
- Push button
- Check box
- Popup
- Scrollable list

Not all these types of objects are needed in one screen layout. The choice depends on your need and your preference.

At this point, you may want to bring forward a dialog screen from the diskette supplied with this book to see this user-built dialog screen. Here are the steps to follow.

1. Select the File menu and **Open** option.

2. Select **Screen** from the Type popup.

3. Select **RENTAL.SCX** and **Open**. The screen layout should look like the following figure.

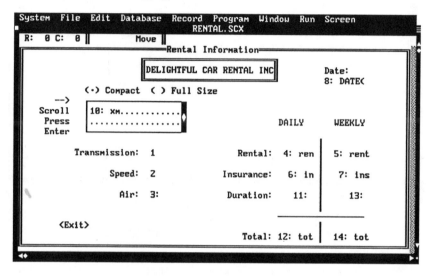

This screen layout is for a rental car firm to answer questions from a prospective customer. The firm offers two sizes of cars, compact and full size. Several models are available in each car size. As you can see, the screen layout displays several items of information on each car model to help a prospective customer decide what model to rent.

Run this screen layout to see how it works. Here are the steps to follow.

1. Select the Close box to close this screen.

2. Select the Program menu and **Do** option.

3. Select **RENTAL.SPR** from the Do Program File list. Notice that the file with extension .SPR is the program file which FoxPro uses to bring the screen alive.

4. Select **Do**. Your screen should now look like the following figure.

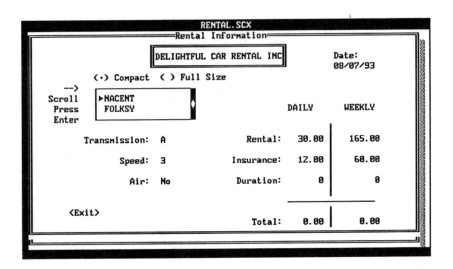

5. Scroll the list if necessary and select the "AGILE" car model. Notice that all information items change to match the selected model.

6. Click on the text area next to "Duration" under the "Daily" column. Type **3**.

   Notice that the total cost of renting "AGILE" for three days appears after your data entry, and the highlight moves to the Duration row of Weekly. Check the result manually.

7. Type **2** and press **Enter** to change the Weekly Duration to 2. Observe the result.

8. Scroll the list to see all the car models in the compact size.

9. Notice that as soon as you move the cursor into the list, all input data and calculated results become zero. This resetting ensures that old information is not displayed to mislead the user.

10. Select **Full Size**.

11. Notice that the screen automatically displays a full size car, "PALACE," on the list, and all input data and calculated results become zero again.

12. Try to scroll the list to display a compact car model while Full Size is on. You cannot click on one! Is the dialog screen intelligent?

13. Select **Exit** when you are ready to exit.

The RENTAL.SCX gives you an idea of how a user can build a dialog screen for real world applications. The Screen Builder makes it easy for a user to build his or her own screens. How about starting to build one for yourself?

THE SCREEN BUILDING PROCESS

In this exercise, you build a dialog screen about stock trading. This screen allows you to select one of two stock exchanges and then select a stock to see the trading information. You can optionally input the number of shares you want to buy at the current price and the screen calculates for you the total cost of the order. You need to use two databases named NATIONAL.DBF and COMMERCE.DBF which contain stock information of the two stock exchanges. The files are on the diskette supplied with this book. You can browse them if you want.

NOTE
In the following screen building process, you can move, resize, and delete Screen Builder objects as you did with Report Writer objects.

You can use the following figure as a guide to design your screen layout.

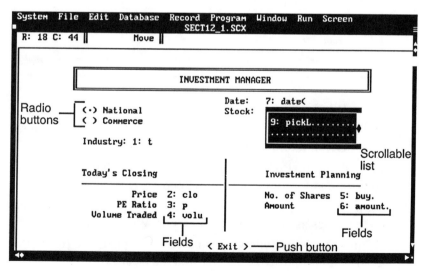

Here are the steps to begin the screen layout.

1. Open the database NATIONAL.DBF.

2. Select the Database menu and **Browse** option to browse this database.

3. Press **Esc** to remove the Browse window when done.

4. Select the File menu and **New** option.

5. Select **Screen** and **OK**. The Screen Design window appears. It is a blank screen.

6. Select the Screen menu and **Screen Layout** option. The Screen Layout dialog appears. See the following figure.

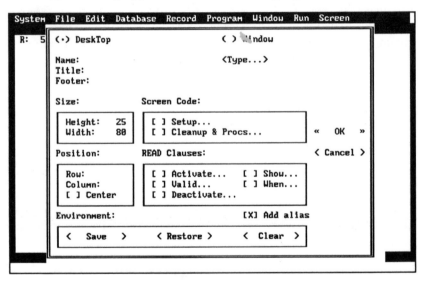

7. Select **Window** (the radio button).

8. Change the Height to 25 (rows) and the Width to 80 (columns). Select **OK** to return to the Screen Design window.

9. Type all the text of headings on the window. Follow the same procedure as for typing text on a Report Layout window.

10. Draw the box around the screen title and the horizontal and vertical lines as you did with the Report Writer.

11. Continue with the following subsections to place the fields, the radio buttons, the scrollable list, and the push button.

PLACING FIELDS IN THE SCREEN LAYOUT In this screen layout, the fields *date( )*, *type*, *close* (closing price of the day), *volume*, *pe*, and *amount* are Say fields. The field *buy* is a Get field. Here are the steps to place the fields.

1. Click on the position for *type* next to "Industry:" on the Screen Design window, or move the cursor to this position. Select the Screen menu and **Field** option. A dialog appears. See the following figure.

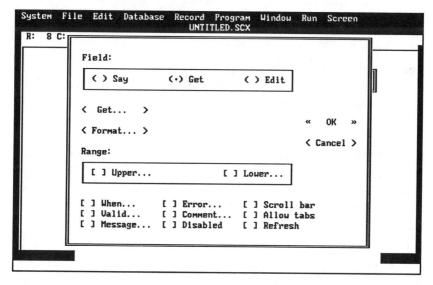

2. Select **Say**. Notice that the check boxes change with your selection.
3. Type **type** in the text area next to Say. . . .
4. Select **Format.** . . . A dialog appears.
5. Type **XXXX** in the text area below Format. Select **OK**.
6. Select **Refresh**. It instructs the Screen Builder to display the latest information of the field in case the value has changed. For example, you may have selected another stock.
7. Select **OK**.
8. Repeat steps 1 through 7 to place the fields *close*, *pe*, *volume*, *buy*, and *amount*. Use the following formats:

close	Say	Numeric	**9999.9**
pe	Say	Numeric	**999.9**

volume	Say	Numeric	**9999999**
buy	Get	Numeric	**9999999**
amount	Say	Numeric	**9999999999**

There is no need to Refresh *buy*.

9. Place *date( )*:

   a. Click on the position for this field on the Screen Design window or move the cursor to this position. Select the Screen menu and **Field** option. A dialog appears.

   b. Select **Say**.

   c. Type **date( )** in the text area.

   d. Select **Refresh**.

   e. Select **Format...** and select **Date** from the dialog. Select **OK**.

   f. Select **OK** to return to the Screen Design window.

CREATING THE RADIO BUTTONS The radio buttons allow you to select either the National Exchange or the Commerce Exchange at runtime. You can switch back and forth as many times as you want, but you cannot select *both* at the same time. Here are the steps to create the radio buttons.

1. Click on the position for the top radio button on the Screen Design window or move the cursor to this position. Select the Screen menu and **Radio Button** option. A dialog appears. See the following figure.

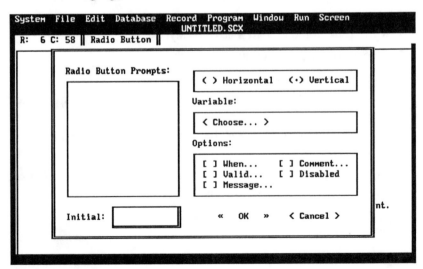

2. Type **National** in the Radio Button Prompts text area.

3. Type **Commerce** on the line below.

4. Click on the text area below Variable. . . or move the cursor to this position. Type **pickR,** the variable name the Screen Builder uses to store the value of the radio button you choose at runtime.

5. Accept "NATIONAL" in the Initial popup. Do nothing. The initial value is the default value displayed at runtime.

6. Accept Vertical. Do nothing. This option arranges the buttons in a vertical line.

7. Select **OK.** Notice that FoxPro has placed the two radio buttons on the Screen Design window.

CREATING THE SCROLLABLE LIST Here are the steps to follow.

1. Click on the position for the top left corner of the list on the Screen Design window, or move the cursor to this position. Select the Screen menu and **List** option. A dialog appears. See the following figure.

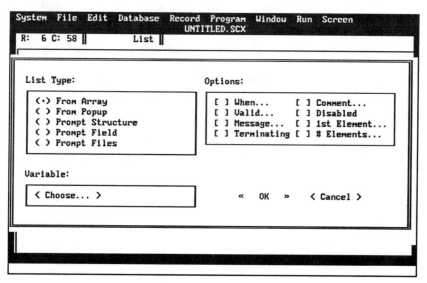

2. Select **Prompt Field**. This option tells the Screen Builder that the list is for displaying a field from a database.

3. Type **stock** in the text area next to Prompt Field.

4. Click on the text area below Variable. . . . Type **pickL,** the variable the Screen Builder uses at runtime to store the value of the data field for display.

5. Select **OK**.

6. Notice that FoxPro has placed the scrollable list on the Screen Design window.

7. Stretch the scrollable list to the right.

    a. With the mouse:

        (1) Press **Ctrl** and click on the object and drag the mouse downward and to the right until the list is the desired size. Release the button.

    b. With the keyboard:

        (1) Move the cursor to the object.

        (2) Press **Ctrl+Spacebar**. The object blinks.

        (3) Press the **Right** and **Down Arrows** to stretch the list until the list is the desired size.

        (4) Press **Enter**. The object stops blinking.

CREATING THE PUSH BUTTON   This push button is to enable you to stop the screen from running when you want to exit the screen. Here are the steps to create the button.

1. Click on the position for this button on the Screen Design window or move the cursor to this position. Select the Screen menu and **Push Button** option. A dialog appears. See the following figure.

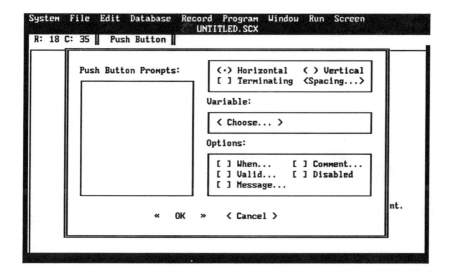

2. Type **Exit** in the Push Button Prompts list text area.

   Notice that if you have more than one button to create, you type the prompts of the buttons in successive lines in this list.

3. Click on the text area below Variable. . . . Type **pickP**, the variable the Screen Builder uses at runtime to store the value of the push button you select.

4. Accept Horizontal. Do nothing. This option arranges the buttons, if more than one, in a horizontal row.

5. Select **Terminating**. This option instructs the Screen Builder to stop the screen from running and return control to the main menu of FoxPro.

6. Select **OK**.

You have created a nice screen. Save it as SECT12_1 to avoid accidental loss of it. You give a final touch to this screen in Section 13 to animate it. Answer **No** and do not save the Environment with the screen.

Section 13

ANIMATING OBJECTS ON SCREEN

FOXPRO COMMANDS

You use FoxPro commands to animate the objects of your dialog screen. A *command* is an instruction written precisely according to the rules (or syntax) of the command language of FoxPro. A command instructs FoxPro to perform the tasks defined in the command. For example, if you want to open the database *course.dbf,* the command is:

USE course

To close all databases, the command is:

CLOSE DATABASES

The syntax must be observed precisely, including the use of punctuation marks (the period, the comma, the semicolon, and so forth). The use of uppercase and lowercase, however, is interchangeable. In this section, we write all command words and filenames in uppercase and all other names (field names and variable names) in lowercase. This style has nothing to do with syntax rules. It is for clarity and ease of checking command writing.

The FoxPro command language is powerful, but the aim of FoxPro is to enable an end-user to use FoxPro with as little command writing (or programming) as possible. To this end, FoxPro has built much programming capability into the interface tools. You need only write a few commands to animate your screen objects. As the set of commands needed is short, FoxPro calls a set of commands for a screen object a *code snippet*.

ADDING CODE SNIPPETS

In the following procedures, type the commands precisely as shown in boldface. Press Enter after typing *each line*. Do *not* use bold style. Do *not* type the line number of each line. The line number is provided for ease of reference in our discussion of the commands. The indentation of some lines is for good readability. You can, in fact, begin a command line at any column. FoxPro ignores all leading and trailing blank spaces in a command line.

VALID CLAUSE OF buy FIELD

1. Double-click on the *buy* field or move the cursor to this position and press **Enter** to open its dialog.

2. Select **Valid**. A small text editing window appears. See the following figure.

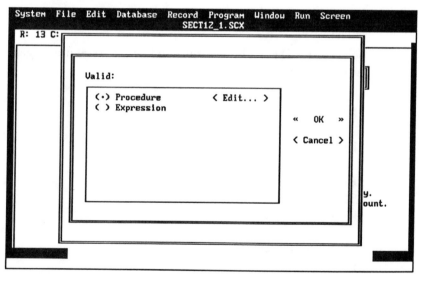

3. Click on the text editing area or move the cursor into it. Type the following code snippet in the window.

```
1    amount = buy * close
2    SHOW GETS OFF
```

4. Select **OK**.

5. Select **OK** to return to the Screen Design window.

CAUTION

Do not press Esc to close the text editing window. FoxPro takes Esc to mean that you want to discard what you have typed, so it does not save the typing.

The following explains the code snippet.

- Line 1 calculates the amount for buying the number of shares determined by *buy* at a price determined by *close*.

- Line 2 instructs FoxPro to redisplay what it gets. This command ensures that FoxPro displays the latest information.

VALID CLAUSE OF RADIO BUTTONS

1. Double-click on either of the radio buttons or move the cursor to this object and press **Enter** to open its dialog.

2. Select **Valid**. The Code Snippet window appears.

3. Open the editing window:

   a. Select **Edit**.

   b. Select **OK**. The Radio Button window closes and a larger editing window appears.

4. Type the following code snippet in the window.

```
1   IF pickR = 1
2          SELECT national
3   ELSE
4          SELECT commerce
5   ENDIF
6   SET ORDER TO type
7   IF pickL <> stock
8          GO TOP
9          pickL = stock
10  ENDIF
11  buy = 0
12  SHOW GETS
```

5. Click on the Close box or select the File menu and **Close** option to close the editing window.

The following explains the code snippet.

- Line 1 tests which radio button is selected at runtime. If *pickR* is 1, the first radio button is selected. If *pickR* is not 1 (the command word ELSE in line 3), the second radio button is selected.
- Line 2 selects the database NATIONAL.DBF for use when *pickR* is 1.
- Line 4 selects the database COMMERCE.DBF for use when *pickR* is not 1.
- Line 5 marks the end of the test which begins with IF in line 1.
- Line 6 instructs FoxPro to arrange the data records alphabetically according to the values stored in the data field *type*. Notice that the SET ORDER TO command is synonymous to selecting Set Order in RQBE.
- Line 7 tests whether the current record for display in the scrollable list is blank or not. If it is (that is, *pickL* <> *stock*), then do lines 8 and 9. The symbol <> means "not equal to."
- Line 8 sets the record pointer to the top record. In other words, make the top record the current record.
- Line 9 copies the value of the data field *stock* of the current record into *pickL* for display.
- Line 11 resets the value of *buy* to zero because the user may have switched from one radio button to the other. The reset ensures that no old quantity is displayed to mislead the user.

WHEN CLAUSE OF SCROLLABLE LIST

1. Double-click on any part of the pick list field, or move the cursor to this object and press **Enter** to open its dialog.
2. Click on **When**. A text editing area appears.
3. Type the following code snippet in the window.
   ```
   1   buy = 0
   2   SHOW GETS
   ```
4. Select **OK** twice to return to the Screen Design window.

FoxPro carries out (executes) the commands in this code snippet whenever the cursor moves into the scrollable list. This is why this clause is called the "When" clause. Line 1 resets the value of *buy* to zero. Line 2 instructs FoxPro to display the latest information. The actions are called for because there is a possibility of the user scrolling the list when the cursor is in the list.

SETUP CODE SNIPPET The Setup code snippet instructs FoxPro as to what preparatory work it should do when it brings the screen layout up and running. Here are the steps to prepare the Setup code snippet.

1. Select the Screen menu and **Screen Layout** option. The Screen Layout dialog appears. Select **Window**.

2. Click on the text area next to Title or move the cursor to this position. Type **My Screen**.

3. Select **Setup**. Select **OK** to bring the text editing window to the front layer of the monitor screen so you can type the code snippet.

4. Type the following code snippet.

```
 1   REGIONAL buy, amount, pickR, pickL, pickP
 2   CLEAR
 3   CLOSE DATABASES
 4   SELECT A
 5   USE national
 6   SELECT B
 7   USE commerce
 8   SELECT national
 9   SET ORDER TO type
10   GO TOP
11   buy = 0
12   amount = 0
13   pickR = 1
14   pickL = stock
15   pickP = 1
```

5. Click on the Close box or select the File menu and **Close** option to close the editing window. The Screen Design window returns.

The following explains the code snippet.

- Line 1 instructs FoxPro to make the variables available for use throughout the entire screen program.

- Line 2 clears the monitor screen to prepare for a start of your screen program.

- Line 3 closes all databases that may be open when you start your screen program, to ensure that they will not interfere with your screen program.

- Line 4 assigns a memory area (called A) for use by NATIONAL.DBF. Line 5 opens this database in the assigned area.

- Line 6 assigns a memory area (called B) for use by COMMERCE.DBF. Line 7 opens this database in the assigned area.

- Line 8 makes NATIONAL.DBF the active database at the start of the screen program.

- Line 9 arranges the records of the active database in the ascending order of the values of the field *type*.

- Line 10 moves the data record pointer in the active database to the top of the file, that is, the first record.

- Lines 11 to 15 assign an initial value to each variable. This is also a way to tell FoxPro the types of the variables, for example, numeric or character.

CLEANUP CODE SNIPPET FoxPro executes this code snippet when you ask to exit your screen at runtime. This code snippet, therefore, should instruct FoxPro to clean up at the time of exit. Here are the steps to prepare the Cleanup code snippet.

1. Select the Screen menu and **Screen Layout** option.
2. Select **Cleanup & Procs**.
3. Select **OK** to bring the text editing window to the front layer of the monitor screen.
4. Type the following code snippet.

   1 **CLEAR**

5. Click on the Close box or select the File menu and **Close** option to close the editing window.

The code snippet clears the current display on the monitor screen to leave a clean screen for the next task.

SAVING, GENERATING, AND RUNNING THE DIALOG SCREEN You need to save the screen file again and then generate the screen program. "Generate" is to convert the screen layout into a FoxPro program which FoxPro uses to run the screen. Foxpro does the programming for you when it generates the program. Here are the steps to follow.

1. Select the File menu and **Save** (not Save As) option. This option saves your present screen by overwriting the existing file SECT12_1.SCX.

2. Select the Program menu and **Generate** option. A dialog appears.

3. Select **Generate**. Wait until generation is done and the cursor reappears.

4. Press **Esc** to close SECT12_1.SCX.

5. Select the Program menu and **Do** option.

6. Select **SECT12_1.SPR** and **Do**. Wait until FoxPro finishes compiling the program. Your dialog screen is then up and running. See the following figure.

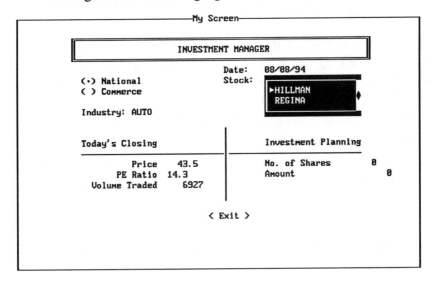

7. Try all the features of your dialog screen to satisfy yourself that the screen *does* work well.

8. Select **Exit** when you want to exit. Observe that the monitor screen is clean and tidy after the exit.

What an amazing screen you have created! You can do more to create a custom menu to run your applications all "under one roof." Shall we move on?

CREATING A CUSTOM MENU SYSTEM

INTRODUCTION

A menu is a productivity tool for you to access frequently used applications quickly. You have used much of FoxPro's menu and no doubt you appreciate how effective it is and how easy to use. You are going to create a custom menu system that works just as well as FoxPro's. Your custom menu system has menu pads and submenus as shown in the following figure.

Focus	Information	Tools	Exit
Data Entry	Investment	Save	
Mailing List	Rental Car	Print Setup	
		Print Report	
		Filer	

THE FOCUS MENU This menu pad has a submenu which offers two options. The Data Entry option calls up a custom screen, REGISTER.SPR, for entering data into SEMINAR.DBF. The Mailing List option calls up the RQBE file SECT10_1.QPR to select criteria for a mailing list. After the RQBE is done, you can print the mailing list through the Tools menu. The file REGISTER.SPR is included on the companion diskette.

TIP: The file REGISTER.SPR is an added illustration. It shows the advantages of using an input screen to enter data into a database. One notable advantage is that the screen enables you to avoid directly typing data into a database record. If you change your mind about the data, you can simply discard them and your data will not get into the database. A second notable advantage is that this screen guards against saving data which are incomplete. These two measures help ensure the integrity of the data in a database. Data integrity is very important in database management.

THE INFORMATION MENU   This menu pad has a submenu which offers two options. The Investment option runs your screen file SECT12_1.SPR about stock information. The Rental Car option runs the file RENTAL.SPR.

THE TOOLS MENU   This menu pad has a submenu which offers four options. The Save option saves the RQBE file after you have changed the selection criteria for a mailing list. The Printer Setup option customizes your printer for a print job. The Print Report option prints the mailing list picked by RQBE. The Filer option lets you manage your files on your computer.

All these four options are taken from FoxPro's own system menu, so this exercise also teaches you how to use the very powerful elements of FoxPro's system menu to build your own menu system.

THE EXIT MENU   This menu pad lets you exit your own menu system in an orderly manner and transfer control back to the FoxPro system menu.

You do four tasks to create the menu system:

- Define menu pads
- Define submenus
- Write code snippets
- Generate program codes

Let us now start to create the menu system.

DEFINING MENU PADS

Follow these steps to define the menu pads.

1. Select the File menu and **New** option.

2. Select **Menu** and **OK**. A dialog appears. Notice that FoxPro has added a Menu pad to the menu bar.

3. Type **\<Focus** in the text area for the first prompt. See the following figure. The symbol \< highlights the letter following it (that is F) at runtime.

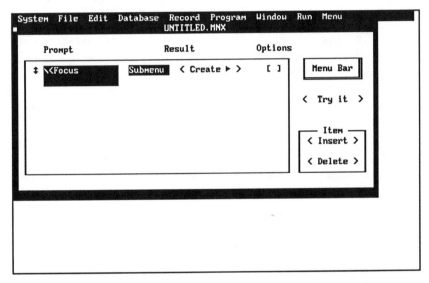

4. Accept Submenu in the Result column.

5. Click on the **Options** check box or move the cursor to this position and press **Spacebar** to select it. A dialog appears. See the following figure.

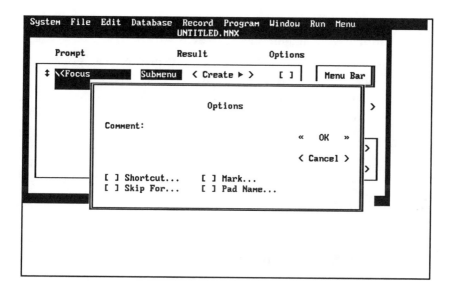

6. Select **Shortcut. . . .** Another dialog appears. See the following figure.

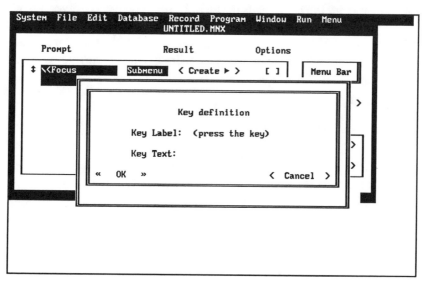

7. Press **Alt+F** to make F of "Focus" the shortcut key. Notice that the keys you pressed are echoed in the dialog. Select **OK** twice to return to the Menu Bar design window.

8. Repeat steps 3 to 7 to define the second prompt. The prompt is \<**Information** and the shortcut key is **Alt+I**.

9. Repeat steps 3 to 7 to define the third prompt. The prompt is \<**Tools** and the shortcut key is **Alt+T**.

10. Click on the fourth prompt text area and type \<**Exit**.

11. Select **Proc** for the Result column.

   a. With the mouse:

     (1) Click on the Result popup and drag the mouse to highlight Proc. Release the button.

   b. With the keyboard:

     (1) Move the cursor to the Result popup.

     (2) Press **Spacebar** to open the popup. Press **Down Arrow** to highlight Proc.

     (3) Press **Spacebar** to close the popup.

12. Repeat steps 5 to 7 to create the shortcut key for Exit. The shortcut key is **Alt+E**.

Now you can try the menu pads defined. Before you try, however, open the Command window and type **ON KEY LABEL ALT+F9 SET SYSMENU TO DEFAULT**. Press **Enter** and hide the Command window. This command enables you to recall the FoxPro's system menu by pressing Alt+F9 if the trial is a failure.

Here are the steps to try your design.

1. Click on **Try It**. Your menu system replaces FoxPro's and a Try It dialog appears.

2. Click on each of the menu pads or press its shortcut key. You see that the selected menu is echoed in the Try It dialog.

3. Select **Done** to return to the Menu Bar design window. FoxPro's system menu returns.

DEFINING SUBMENUS

Follow these steps to define the submenus.

1. Double-click on **Create** of the Focus line, or move the cursor to this position and press **Enter**. A submenu design window appears.

2. Notice that the current menu name in the Menu Level popup has changed from Menu Bar to Focus.

3. Type **\\<Data Entry** in the first prompt.

4. Select **Proc** for the Result column.

5. Repeat steps 3 and 4 for the second prompt. The prompt is **\\<Mailing List**. The Result is **Proc**.

6. Open the Menu Level popup and select **Menu Bar** to return to the Menu Bar design window.

7. Repeat steps 1 to 6 for the next two menu pads, Information and Tools. Use the following details:

Menu Pad	Submenu Option Prompt	Result
Information	**\\<Investment**	Procedure
Information	**Rental \\<Car**	Procedure
Tools	**\\<Save**	Bar #
Tools	**\\<Printer Setup**	Bar #
Tools	**Print \\<Report**	Bar #
Tools	**\\<Filer**	Bar #

Remember that there is no submenu for Exit.

8. Try your submenus with Try It.

9. Select **Menu Bar** from the Menu Level popup to return to the Menu Bar design window.

WRITING CODE SNIPPETS

Follow these steps to write the code snippets for the Data Entry submenu.

1. Make sure that the Menu Level popup displays Menu Bar. Click on **Edit** of the Focus line, or move the cursor to this position and press **Enter**. The Focus submenu design window returns.

2. Click on **Create** of Data Entry, or move the cursor to this position and press **Enter** to open the text editing window.

3. Type **DO REGISTER.SPR** and press **Enter**.

4. Select the Close box, or select the File menu and **Close** option to close the editing window. The submenu design window returns. Notice that the Create push button has now changed to Edit.

5. Repeat steps 2 to 4 for the Mailing List line and type the code snippet **MODIFY QUERY SECT10_1.QPR.**

6. Select **Menu Bar** from the Menu Level popup to return to the Menu Bar design window.

7. Repeat steps 1 to 4 for the Investment line and the Rental Car line of the Information submenu with the following code snippets.

Menu Pad	Submenu	Code Snippet
Information	Investment	**DO SECT12_1.SPR**
Information	Rental Car	**DO RENTAL.SPR**

8. Select **Menu Bar** from the Menu Level popup to return to the Menu Bar. Select **Edit** of the Tools line. The Tools submenu returns.

9. Type the following code snippets in the text area (to the right of the Result column) of the appropriate submenu bar of the Tools submenu. Press **Enter** at the end of each line of code snippet.

Menu Pad	Submenu Bar	Code Snippet
Tools	Save	**_MFI_SAVE**
Tools	Printer Setup	**_MFI_SETUP**
Tools	Print Report	**_MDA_REPRT**
Tools	Filer	**_MST_FILER**

10. Select **Menu Bar** from the Menu Level popup to return to the Menu Bar.

11. Select **Create** of the Exit line. Type the following code snippet in the editing window. Press **Enter** after typing each line.

CLEAR ALL
CLEAR
SET SYSMENU TO DEFAULT

12. Close the text editing window to return to the Menu Bar design window.

GENERATING PROGRAM CODE

You have completed the design of your custom menu system. Save it as MYMENU. Follow these steps to generate the program codes and run the program.

1. Select the Program menu and **Generate** option. A dialog appears. Everything in the dialog is fine. Select **Generate**. Wait until FoxPro completes the generation.
2. Press **Esc** to close the Menu Bar design window.
3. Select the Program menu and **Do** option.
4. Select **MYMENU.MPR**. Select **Do**. Now your menu system is up and running and replaces the FoxPro system menu. See the following figure.

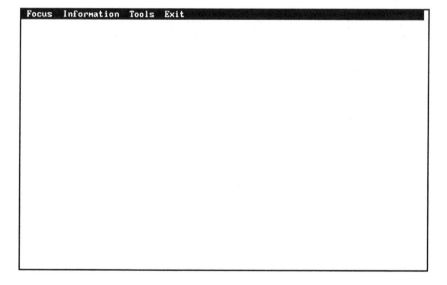

5. Try the menu pads and options and enjoy your splendid work.
6. Select **Exit** to return to the FoxPro system menu when done.

You have accomplished so much! Take a break. Select the File menu and **Exit** option. FoxPro closes down in good order.

WHAT NEXT?

You have successfully graduated from a very rigorous self-training course. You have learned to:

- Create databases
- Enter and edit data records
- Use the Browse window
- Retrieve data by RQBE to provide specific information
- Use the Report Writer in a stand-alone situation
- Use the Report Writer together with RQBE
- Do queries using relational databases
- Prepare calculations using data fields and variables
- Create a dialog screen using the Screen Builder and code snippets
- Create your custom menu system
- Use box and line graphic features

When you look at this long list of accomplishments, you should have no difficulty in giving yourself recognition that you can use FoxPro competently as an end-user. You have also prepared yourself for more advanced learning.

If you want to learn more about FoxPro, you may consider the following suggestions:

- Create your own examples so you can have more practice.
- Use FoxPro in your work. Proficiency comes through practice.
- Study *FoxPro User's Guide* supplied with the FoxPro software.
- Study some of the examples in the FOXPRO25\TUTORIAL directory.

Appendix A

COMPANION DISKETTE

The diskette contains files that you can use for your exercises. You can find the instructions for using these files in the appropriate sections of this book.

Copy these files to a subdirectory named FOXPRO25\WKFILES. For instructions to create the subdirectory and copy the files, see Section 3, CREATING A WORK FILE SUBDIRECTORY and COPYING COMPANION DISKETTE TO WKFILES SUBDIRECTORY.

Appendix B

USING THE FILER

The Filer option is a FoxPro utility to help you manage your disks. You can reach Filer by selecting the System menu and the Filer option. The Filer window looks like the following figure.

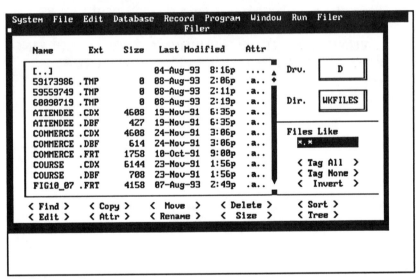

As you can see from the push buttons in the window, Filer deals with DOS operations such as deleting and renaming files. An error in these operations can ruin your files. Therefore, you must use Filer very carefully. If you are not sure what to do, try Filer first with some files which you are going to scrap.

Before you select a push button, you must select (tag) the target file. You can tag several files and then select one push button to operate on all the tagged files. Again, it is prudent to do one file at a time rather than several files in one operation.

The following are Filer procedures which may be useful to beginners. The file to be copied, moved, renamed, or deleted must be closed.

CHANGE DRIVE

1. With the mouse:

    a. Click on the **Drv.** popup, drag the mouse to highlight the target drive, then release the button.

2. With the keyboard:

    a. Move the cursor to the Drv. popup, then press **Spacebar** to open it.

    b. Press **Down Arrow** to the target drive, and then press **Spacebar**.

CHANGE DIRECTORY

1. With the mouse:

    a. Click on the **Dir.** popup, drag the mouse to highlight the target directory, then release the button.

2. With the keyboard:

    a. Move the cursor to the Dir. popup, then press **Spacebar** to open it.

    b. Press **Down Arrow** to the target directory, and then press **Spacebar**.

TAG AND UNTAG A FILE

1. Tag a file.

    a. With the mouse:

        (1) Drag the Thumb of the file list until the desired filename is in view. Click on the filename to select it.

    b. With the keyboard:

        (1) Move the cursor into the list.

        (2) Press **Up** or **Down Arrow** to highlight the desired file. Press **Spacebar** to select it.

2. Click on **Tag None,** or move the cursor to this position and press **Enter** to untag a tagged file.

TIP: If the target file is highlighted, you can untag the file by pressing Shift+Spacebar.

TAG AND UNTAG MULTIPLE FILES

1. Drag the Thumb of the file list until the first of the desired file is in view. Click on the file to select it.
2. Press **Shift+Down Arrow** to highlight all the files to be tagged, or press and hold Shift and click on the target files.
3. Click on **Tag None** to untag the tagged files.

COPY   This push button copies a tagged file to another directory, say D:\. The copied file has the same filename as the source file which remains intact.

1. Tag the source file.
2. Select **Copy.** A dialog appears. See the following figure.

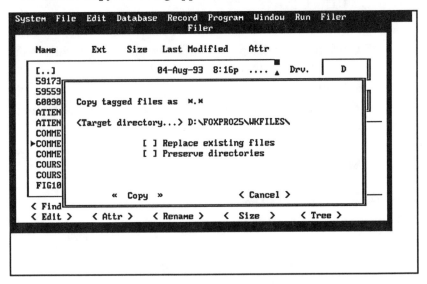

3. Move the cursor to the text area next to Target directory and type **D:\.**
4. Select **Copy.**
5. Select **Tag None** to untag the tagged file.

MOVE This push button acts exactly the same way as Copy, except that after the move, the source file no longer exists in the current directory.

RENAME This push button changes the name of the tagged file to the new name given by you. The file remains in the current directory.

1. Tag the file.
2. Select **Rename**. A dialog appears. See the following figure.

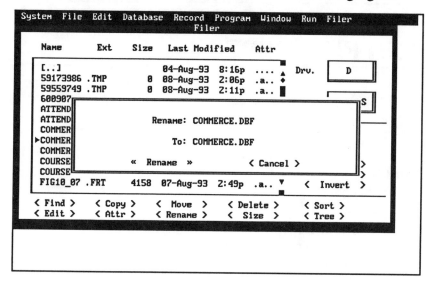

3. Move the cursor to the text area next to "To:" and type the new name.
4. Select **Rename**.

DELETE This push button deletes the tagged file. After deletion, the file no longer exists. Before deletion, FoxPro asks you to confirm or cancel the operation. Select the push button to confirm or cancel as you desire.

Appendix C

SUMMARY OF SPECIAL KEYS AND FILE TYPES

SUMMARY OF SPECIAL KEYS

The following is a summary of the special keys which may be useful to beginners.

Key	Effect
Ctrl+D	Invoke the DO command
Ctrl+W	Exit current editing window and save edited data
Ctrl+F2	Display the Command window
Esc	Cancel the current step without saving the changes made
F1	Display online Help
F3	Invoke the LIST command
F4	Display the current directory
F5	Display the database structure
F8	Invoke the DISPLAY command
F9	Invoke the APPEND command

FILE TYPES

Filename Ext.	File Type
.cdx	Compound index
.dbf	Database
.fpt	Memo file associated with a database
.frx	Report design
.prg	Program
.lbx	Label
.qpr	Query
.scx	Screen design
.spr	Screen program
.spx	Compiled screen program
.mnx	Menu design
.mpr	Menu program
.txt	Text
.vue	View

Appendix D

GLOSSARY

Acronym	An abbreviation coined from a name or a phrase. Example: "DOS" is an acronym for "Disk Operating System."
Active window	The window on the front layer of the computer monitor where a visible action can take place.
Alias	An additional name given to a database for such purposes as allocating work space to the database in the computer's memory.
AND	A logical operator that returns a "true" result only if the two parameters (operands) joined by AND are both true.
Average	The arithmetic mean of a group of numbers.
Band	A line or group of lines in a report layout which presents data in a manner predefined by the Report Writer. There are seven types of bands: Title, Page Header, Group Header, Detail, Group Footer, Page Footer, and Summary.
Browse	To display data of a database on the monitor.
Cancel	To stop the current activity being performed by a computer program, and usually to return to the preceding activity of the program.

Character	Any printable symbol that can be found on the computer keyboard. A blank space is also a character.
Character field	See *Data field.*
Check box	The symbol [ ] used in a FoxPro dialog for the user to interact with FoxPro at the location of the symbol.
Choose	To select an option from a menu, a dialog, and so forth.
Clause	A set of FoxPro commands which is usually used to specify how another command should be performed.
Cleanup code	A clause(s) of commands used for performing house-cleaning functions near the end of a FoxPro application. It may also contain procedures.
Clear	To remove the data being displayed on the monitor.
Click	To press the left button of the mouse once and then release the button.
Close	To close the active window.
Close box	The button at the top left corner of a FoxPro system window. When selected, it closes the window.
Code snippet	A short set of commands built into a FoxPro program to enable a menu, a push button, and so forth to perform certain tasks.
Command	An instruction written according to certain syntax for the computer to perform a task. A command begins with a verb. Example: CLOSE DATABASES.
Context-sensitive	Responding to a request for Help information at runtime such that the Help information relates directly to the situation where help is needed.

Control click	To press and hold down the Ctrl key, then press the left button of the mouse, and then release the Ctrl key and the button.
Control device	A generic name given to a symbol used in a FoxPro dialog to enable the user to interact with FoxPro. Examples are: the check box, the push button, the radio button, the Thumb, and so forth.
Control key	The key that is usually denoted by the symbol "Ctrl" on the keyboard and by the symbol ^ on the monitor.
Data	Textual materials, numbers, figures, and graphics used for providing factual information or for input to a computer program.
Data field	A space with a defined size and type in a database structure for storing data. There are seven types of data fields: character, date, float, logical, memo, numeric, and general.
Data grouping	Arranging data of a database into groups according to some criteria.
Data table	See *database*.
Data type	See *Data field*.
Database	A body of data organized in a systematic manner and applied in a computer-based system. Also called a *data table*.
Database management	To create, maintain, update, use, and retrieve data of a database(s) according to designed processes.
Database structure	The framework of a database defining the number of data fields, the type and size of each field, and the indexing of fields.
Default	An option in a computer program selected automatically by the program if the user does not override the selection.

Default push button	The push button can be selected by pressing the Ctrl+Enter key, regardless of the current position of the cursor.
Delete	(1) To erase a character from a text by pressing the Del or the Backspace key. (2) To erase a file from a directory. (3) To mark a data record in a database for deletion.
Deselect	To cancel the "selected" status of an object in a report layout or a screen layout.
Detail band	See *Band*.
Dialog	A special FoxPro window containing control devices to enable the user to interact with FoxPro.
Dimmed	Dimly lighted data field names, filenames, menu options, and so forth, indicating that these features are not applicable at the current moment.
Directory	A list of files grouped together logically in a computer disk. Every file in a disk must belong to one directory or another.
DOS	The acronym for "Disk Operating System" which is a software for managing the operations of a computer's memory and accessories: the keyboard, the mouse, the monitor, and so forth.
Double-click	To click the left button of the mouse twice in rapid succession.
Drag	To click and hold down the left button of the mouse, then roll the mouse to move the cursor to the target position, and then release the button.
Edit	To modify existing data in a database or in a text file, and so forth.
Expression	A word, a variable, or an arithmetic formula used for representing a value.

Expression Builder	A FoxPro facility which helps the user to compose an expression for incorporation into an application.
Field	See *Data field*.
File type	The type of a file determined according to the file contents. Examples are: database, report, screen, and so forth. The file type must match the filename extension.
Font	A typographic term referring to the size and typeface of a set of characters.
Format	A specification for the type, the size, the spacing arrangements, and so forth of data in input/output.
Function	A mathematic calculation, for example, the sum or the average of a group of numbers.
General field	See *data field*. A general field is for storing graphic data.
Group band	See *Band*.
Group footer/header	See *Band*.
Hide	To move the active window to the background so it becomes invisible. A hidden window is not closed and can be moved forward again.
Highlighted	The opposite of *Dimmed*.
Hot key	The single highlighted character in a prompt of a menu, a push button, and so forth. Pressing the hot key of an option selects the option.
Index	A logical means used in a FoxPro database to mark a data field so that data records can be arranged in an ascending or descending order of the indexed field. FoxPro uses an index as a location finder to locate target records promptly.
Initialize	To give a value to a variable prior to the variable being used.

Interactive	Communicating between the computer and the user through the monitor, the keyboard, and the mouse.
Interface	A generic name given to FoxPro's devices for user interaction with FoxPro. These devices include menus, dialogs, windows, and so forth.
Logical field	See *Data field.*
Logical operator	An operator used in an expression for evaluating data according to Boolean logic. The operators AND, OR, and NOT are logical operators.
Menu	A list of options for a program user to choose from so that the program may perform the chosen task.
Menu Builder	One of FoxPro's power tools for building custom menu systems.
Nested grouping	To organize the reporting of data by groups; one group being embedded within another group.
NOT	A logical operator that returns a "true" result if the parameter (operand) preceded by NOT is not true.
Numeric field	See *Data field.*
Object	A string of text, a graphic, a data field, or a variable entered on the Report Design window or the Screen Design window. An object has certain characteristics given by FoxPro.
Option	A choice among available alternatives in a menu or a dialog.
OR	A logical operator that returns a "true" result if one of the two parameters (operands) joined by OR is true.
PACK	A FoxPro command which physically deletes records in a database that are marked for deletion.
Page footer/header	See *Band.*

Page layout	The design of a page made with the Report Writer specifying such features as page length and width, top and bottom margins, and so forth.
Popup	A menu which appears on selection of a popup control in a dialog.
Procedure	A subprogram of a controlling program.
Program	A file containing commands, data, and text such that the contents of the file can be executed by a software such as FoxPro, in a logical sequence.
Prompt	A word or phrase indicating the task to be performed by a menu, a popup option, a push button, and so forth. Also a message displayed on the monitor to advise the user of the response expected from him or her.
Push button	The symbol < > used in a FoxPro dialog for the user to interact with FoxPro at the location of the symbol.
Query	A search for data in a database according to some search criteria.
Radio button	The symbol ( ) used in a FoxPro dialog for the user to interact with FoxPro at the location of the symbol.
Record	A unit of storage in a database. Each record contains the fields defined in the structure of the database.
Relational databases	Two databases logically joined together by a data field that is common to both databases. The record in one database and the record in the other that have the same value for the common field are then considered logically as being one single record.
Relational operators	An operator that compares two values to determine which is larger, smaller, equal, and so forth.

Report layout	A design of a report format prepared with FoxPro's Report Writer. The report layout is used to produce an actual data report.
Report Writer	A FoxPro "power tool" which enables the user to prepare a report layout without writing program codes.
Runtime	The moment in which a program is running.
RQBE	The acronym for "Relational Query By Example." A FoxPro "power tool" which enables the user to do queries efficiently and without writing program codes.
Screen Builder	A FoxPro "power tool" which enables the user to prepare a custom dialog with the minimum writing of program codes.
Scrollable list	A window used in a FoxPro dialog to display a list of filenames, data fields, and so forth. The display can be scrolled upward and downward if the list is longer than the height of the display window.
Select	(1) To make a choice among available alternatives in menus, dialogs, and so forth. (2) To select an object in a Report Design window or a Screen Design window for a subsequent operation. A selected object becomes highlighted.
Setup code	A clause(s) of FoxPro commands used for performing some preparatory tasks, for example, opening a file, prior to activating the main functions of a FoxPro application.
Size control	A dot symbol at the bottom right corner of a FoxPro system window which can interact with the mouse to change the size of the window.
SQL	The acronym for "Structured Query Language" which is a set of powerful and concise commands designed for doing queries.

Style   The description of certain features of the font, such as italic or boldface.

Sum   The total of a group of numbers.

Summary band   See *Band*.

Syntax   The rules for using a computer programming language.

System window   The universal window used by FoxPro. It has several typical features such as a window title bar and buttons for handling the operation of the window.

Thumb   A diamond-shaped symbol on the right border or bottom border of a scrollable list. It shows the position of the portion of the list on display relative to the total length of the list. You can drag the Thumb upward and downward to scroll the list.

Title band   See *Band*.

Variable   A space in the computer memory for storing a value. The value can change as the program runs. A variable must have a unique name.

Window   A screen display of a given design.

Zoom control   A button at the top right corner of a FoxPro system window. Clicking this button enlarges the current window to occupy the entire monitor screen. Clicking this button again will reduce the window to its previous size.

Index

Other Books from Wordware Publishing, Inc.

Illustrated Series
Illustrated AutoCAD (Release 10)
Illustrated AutoCAD (Release 11)
Illustrated AutoSketch 2.0
Illustrated Borland C++ 3.1
Illustrated C Programming (ANSI)
 (2nd Ed.)
Illustrated DacEasy Accounting 4.2
Illustrated dBASE III Plus
Illustrated dBASE IV 1.1
Illustrated Enable/OA
Illustrated MS-DOS 5.0
Illustrated Novell NetWare
 2.x/3.x Software
Illustrated PageMaker 4.0
Illustrated Q&A 4.0
Illustrated QBasic for MS-DOS 5.0
Illustrated UNIX System V
Illustrated WordPerfect 5.1
Illustrated WordPerfect for
 Windows

General and Advanced Topics
111 Clipper Functions
The Complete Communications
 Handbook
Financial Modeling using
 Lotus 1-2-3
Graphic User Interface
 Programming with C
Graphics Programming with
 Turbo Pascal
Novell NetWare: Advanced
 Techniques and Applications
Programming On-Line Help
 using C++
Understanding 3COM Networks

Advanced Networking Series
Demystifying SNA
Demystifying TCP/IP
Integrating TCP/IP into SNA
Networking with Windows NT

Popular Applications Series
Build Your Own Computer
Cost Control Using Lotus 1-2-3
Desktop Publishing Handbook
Desktop Publishing with Word 2.0
 for Windows
Desktop Publishing with
 WordPerfect
Desktop Publishing with
 WordPerfect for Windows
Learn AmiPro 3.0 in a Day
Learn AutoCAD in a Day
Learn AutoCAD 12 in a Day
Learn C in Three Days
Learn CorelDRAW! in a Day
Learn dBASE Programming
 in a Day
Learn DOS in a Day
Learn DOS 6.0 in a Day
Learn DOS 6.2 in a Day
Learn DrawPerfect in a Day
Learn Excel for Windows
 in a Day (Ver. 3.0 & 4.0)
Learn FoxPro 2.5 in a Day
Learn FoxPro for Windows
 in a Day
Learn Freelance Graphics for
 Windows in a Day
Learn Generic CADD 6.0 in a Day
Learn Harvard Graphics 3.0
 in a Day
Learn Lotus 1-2-3 in a Day

Call Wordware Publishing, Inc. for names of the bookstores in your area
(214) 423-0090

Other Books from Wordware Publishing, Inc.

Popular Applications Series (Cont.)

Learn Lotus 1-2-3 Ver. 2.4 in a Day
Learn Lotus 1-2-3 Rel. 4 for
  Windows in a Day
Learn MS Access 2.0 in a Day
Learn Microsoft Assembler
  in a Day
Learn MS Excel 5.0 for Windows
  in a Day
Learn Microsoft Works in a Day
Learn Microsoft Works 3.0
  in a Day
Learn Norton Utilities in a Day
Learn Novell NetWare Software
  in a Day
Learn OS/2 in a Day
Learn PageMaker 4.0 in a Day
Learn PageMaker 5.0 in a Day
Learn PAL in a Day
Learn PAL 4.5 in a Day
Learn Paradox 4.0 in a Day
Learn Paradox 4.5 in a Day
Learn Pascal in Three Days
Learn PC-Tools 8.0 in a Day
Learn PlanPerfect in a Day
Learn Q&A 4.0 in a Day
Learn Quattro Pro 4.0 in a Day
Learn Quattro Pro 5.0 in a Day
Learn Quicken in a Day
Learn Timeslips for Windows
  in a Day
Learn Turbo Assembler
  Programming in a Day
Learn Ventura 4.0 in a Day
Learn Windows in a Day
Learn Windows NT in a Day
Learn Word 2.0 for Windows
  in a Day
Learn Word 6.0 for Windows
  in a Day
Learn WordPerfect in a Day
  (2nd Edition)

Popular Applications Series (Cont.)

Learn WordPerfect 6.0 in a Day
Learn WordPerfect 5.2 for
  Windows in a Day
Learn WordPerfect 6.0 for
  Windows in a Day
Learn WordPerfect Presentations
  in a Day
Moving from WordPerfect for
  DOS to WordPerfect for
  Windows
Object-Oriented Programming
  using Turbo C++
Programming Output Drivers
  using Borland C++
Repair and Upgrade Your Own PC
WordPerfect 6.0 Survival Skills
Write TSRs Now
Write Your Own Programming
  Language using C++

At A Glance Series

CorelDRAW! for Windows at a
  Glance
FoxPro 2.5 at a Glance
FoxPro for Windows at a Glance
Lotus 1-2-3 Rel. 4 for Windows
  at a Glance
Microsoft Excel 5.0 for Windows
  at a Glance
Microsoft Windows at a Glance
Paradox 4.5 at a Glance
Quattro Pro 5.0 at a Glance
Quattro Pro 4.0 for Windows at a
  Glance
Quattro Pro 5.0 for Windows
  at a Glance
Word 2.0 for Windows at a Glance
WordPerfect 6.0 at a Glance
WordPerfect 6.0 for Windows
  at a Glance

Call Wordware Publishing, Inc. for names of the bookstores in your area
(214) 423-0090

Regional Books From Wordware

100 Days in Texas: The Alamo Letters
by Wallace O. Chariton

At Least 1836 Things You Ought to Know About Texas but Probably Don't
by Doris Miller

Classic Clint: The Laughs and Times of Clint Murchison, Jr.
by Dick Hitt

Country Savvy: Survival Tips for Farmers, Ranchers, and Cowboys
by Reed Blackmon

Critter Chronicles
by Jim Dunlap

Defense of a Legend: Crockett and the de la Peña Diary
Bill Groneman

Dirty Dining: A Cookbook, and More, for Lovers
by Ginnie Siena Bivona

Don't Throw Feathers at Chickens: A Collection of Texas Political Humor
by Charles Herring, Jr. and Walter Richter

Exploring the Alamo Legends
by Wallace O. Chariton

From an Outhouse to the Whitehouse
by Wallace O. Chariton

The Great Texas Airship Mystery
by Wallace O. Chariton

Kingmakers
by John R. Knaggs

The Last Great Days of Radio
by Lynn Woolley

Outlaws and Petticoats
by Ann Ruff

Rainy Days in Texas Funbook
by Wallace O. Chariton

Recovery: A Directory to Texas Substance Abuse Treatment Facilities
Edited by Linda Manning-Miller

San Antonio Uncovered
by Mark Louis Rybczyk

Slitherin' 'Round Texas
by Jim Dunlap

Spirits of San Antonio and South Texas
by Docia Schultz Williams and Reneta Byrne

Texas Highway Humor
by Wallace O. Chariton

Texas Politics in My Rearview Mirror
Waggoner Carr and Byron Varner

Texas Tales Your Teacher Never Told You
by Charles F. Eckhardt

Texas Wit and Wisdom
by Wallace O. Chariton

That Cat Won't Flush
by Wallace O. Chariton

That Old Overland Stagecoaching
by Eva Jolene Boyd

They Don't Have to Die
by Jim Dunlap

This Dog'll Hunt
by Wallace O. Chariton

To The Tyrants Never Yield
by Kevin R. Young

A Trail Rider's Guide to Texas
by Mary Elizabeth Sue Goldman

Unsolved Texas Mysteries
by Wallace O. Chariton

Western Horse Tales
Edited by Don Worcester

Call Wordware Publishing, Inc. for names of the bookstores in your area
(214) 423-0090